PASSION
AND
REASON

PASSION
AND
REASON

Womenviews of Christian Life

GRACE D. CUMMING LONG

Westminster/John Knox Press
Louisville, Kentucky

Scripture quotations from the New Revised Standard Version of the Bible are copyright © 1989 by the Division of Christian Education of the National Council of the Churches of Christ in the U.S.A., and are used by permission.

Excerpt on pp. 28–29 from María Teresa Porcile S., pp. 33–34 in "Water in the Slums," in *New Eyes for Reading: Biblical and Theological Reflections by Women From the Third World,* ed. John S. Pobee and Bärbel von Wartenberg-Potter (Geneva: WCC, 1986). Copyright © WCC Publications, World Council of Churches, Geneva, Switzerland. Reprinted by permission of the publisher.

Excerpt on pp. 41–42 from *Touching Our Strength: The Erotic as Power and the Love of God* by Carter Heyward. Copyright © 1989 by Carter Heyward. Reprinted by permission of HarperCollins Publishers.

First edition

Published by Westminster/John Knox Press
Louisville, Kentucky

This book is printed on acid-free paper that meets the American National Standards Institute Z39.48 standard. ∞

PRINTED IN THE UNITED STATES OF AMERICA
9   8   7   6   5   4   3   2   1

Library of Congress Cataloging–in–Publication Data

Long, Grace D. Cumming.
    Passion and reason : womenviews of Christian life / Grace D.
Cumming Long. — 1st ed.
        p.   cm.
    Includes bibliographical references.
    ISBN 0–664–25408–X (alk. paper)
    1. Feminist theology.   2. Feminist ethics.   I. Title.
BT83.55.L66   1993
230'.082—dc20   93–19481

In memory of
my grandmothers:
Grace Darling Cumming
and
Lula May Powell Towler

Contents

Acknowledgments

Many people have contributed to this book, although none of them can be held accountable for its shortcomings. *This* book could not have been written were it not for Barbara Robeson and Dr. Ella Robeson, who were instrumental in my becoming a public health nurse, or the twenty or so nurses with whom I worked, or the hundreds of families whom I served. I have been blessed by all of them. My colleagues and students at Pacific Lutheran University, Princeton Theological Seminary, and New York Theological Seminary spurred me on. My mentors, Marjorie B. Chambers and Edward LeRoy Long, Jr., were partners along the way; their reading, suggestions, and encouragement were important, and I am thankful. The Rev. Theodore Evans and the Women's Study Group at St. Paul's Church in Stockbridge, Massachusetts, read an early version of the manuscript, and their helpful suggestions have been incorporated into the finished work. I am especially indebted to Martha Ellen Stortz, who was able to see better than I what I was doing in the book. Her extensive comments and insightful suggestions had an important impact on the final version of the manuscript. I deeply appreciate the library assistance of Virginia Gilmore and Josepha Cook. The helpful suggestions of Marion D. Banzhaf, Coordinator of the New Jersey Women and AIDS Network, and Rosemary Lillis made chapters 4 and 10 more accurate and current. Alexa Smith, editor and friend, has enriched me greatly in the process of moving from proposal to final manuscript. Finally, I am grateful for the grace and skill with which Katy Monk and Danielle Alexander at Westminster/John Knox Press and copy editor Hank Schlau have undertaken the arduous task of getting from manuscript to book.

1

UNCONVENTIONAL MIRRORS

Mirrors

Historically, the symbol for women has been a hand-held mirror, rendered graphically as a circle or oval above a cross (♀). This mirror has imaged women both as objects to be looked upon and used and also as occupiers of the home, particularly the bedroom. Thus the mirror symbol has stereotyped and located women. Today, women are redefining their roles and relocating their spheres of influence. In their mirrors women now see images not of objects but of subjects, situated not in the bedroom but in the whole world. Women see images of themselves and one another as creators of new life, designers of healthier social organizations, thinkers of different ideas, and actors in unlimited spheres.

At the same time, more and more women are finding that their biologically and culturally determined roles — as givers and nurturers of new life, as caretakers for dependent persons, as builders of communities, and as enablers of one another — provide rich resources for reinterpreting human life in every dimension. Women's perspectives yield understandings of life that diverge from conventional ways of thinking, which have been derived almost entirely from men's experiences and perceptions.

This book holds up women's unconventional mirrors as sources for seeing Christian life in alternative theological and ethical dimensions. Such an approach is based on my conviction that women's contexts and experiences are, in and of themselves, valid loci of revelation for understanding God in relation to human life. Repeatedly, I am frustrated by women who argue for a feminist view of theology or ethics and seek support or validation for their arguments in the theology and ethics, psychology and philosophy, sociology and anthropology of men. Earlier women writers had so few women's books to draw upon that they had to glean from men's work whatever was liberating and healing for women. Today, however, there is a plethora of books, essays, and articles by women in every field of academic study; and many if not most of these writings take a decidedly women's perspective on what has been a male-defined world. Therefore, I can turn with confidence to women's writings as sufficient resources for an ethical understanding of Christian life.

1

Nevertheless, for women who want to remain within the Christian community, the images and ideas that are mirrored cannot be limited totally to the contexts and experiences of women. Christianity's written and structural heritage, from the Bible to the twentieth-century church, has been created almost entirely by men. The alternative voices of women throughout the tradition are being recovered, and these can be sources for women's perspectives on Christianity. Yet this is not enough. Women have to read inventive meanings into the male-defined Bible by bringing different interpretive frameworks to bear on the texts. In this way, women can find in biblical texts messages that were neither intended by male writers nor recognized by male editors. What better confirmation of the living God who engages us in the texts? Traditional biblical scholarship has been based on the belief that pure and objective interpretation is possible; but more and more Christian scholars are realizing that our reading of all texts is shaped by our cultural and experiential lenses. Thus women's diverse perspectives on the male texts of the Bible, seen in the mirrors of women's lives, can reflect womenviews of Christian life.

Womenviews of Human Life for Ethics

I use the word "womenviews" for many reasons. I use the term with my own sense of what it means to be woman — artist, daughter, educator, ethicist, granddaughter, grandmother, mother, nurse, scholar, spouse, volunteer (I have listed these in alphabetical order because I cannot prioritize). I use "womenviews" in protest against the narrow views of much early feminism that denigrated my enriching years as mother (and now grandmother), my deeply satisfying service as nurse, and my creative and empowering growth in voluntary activities. I use the term to encompass the thinking of American women of African, Asian, and Hispanic heritage who cannot find space for themselves in feminism. I use it to include women in Africa, Asia, and Latin America who value women more than feminism, who affirm motherhood and find metaphors for theology and ethics in birth and parenting. I use "womenviews" on behalf of mothers on welfare whom I served as a public health nurse. Memories of their alienated and oppressed situation remain very painful for me. My use of "womenviews," however, also includes feminist views. I am affirming what feminism has given me. Indeed, without the earlier work of feminists I could not be where I am vocationally or intellectually. To speak of womenviews means I am listening to many diverse women while being true to my own identity and insights.

Note that I use the term *"women*views" and not *"woman*views." I do not find in women's lives or writings a singular experience or perception of life. Rather, I find that women's lives are different according to their culture and their socioeconomic status, so they offer a plurality of views.

This great diversity in women's lived realities is reflected in their writings. I find in women's perspectives a rich array of images with which I can reflect on my own views of Christian life. Yet even as I recognize this variety, I also find in women's perspectives recurrent threads or points of connection that provide enough common ground to think in terms of "womenviews" as something recognizably distinct from "menviews" or "humanviews."

When I speak of "womenviews of human life," I am not referring to women's lives in particular. Rather, womenviews bring a particular perspective to the formulation of a Christian view of being human, female and male. Moreover, I use the terminology "being human" or "human life" rather than the traditional "human nature" because I am more concerned about concrete relationships than abstract essences. I do recognize that who and what we are shapes our relationships, yet it may be as impossible to know the essence of ourselves as it is to know God's essence. As Christians we can know only what our lived experiences with God and one another convey to us about ourselves. These experiences of God and self are known in our interactions with one another more than through self-reflecting or other-objectifying abstractions.

No attempt is made here to define human life in its entirety. I seek *womenviews of human life for ethics* in order to lift up aspects of being human that are revealed by women's perspectives to be important for faithful Christian life. The purpose is to present some of the realities of human life that have been ignored, denigrated, or distorted, to explore experiences of human creativity and creatureliness that womenviews see as important for Christian ethics.

Christian womenviews of human life for ethics are necessarily theological views. Christian ethics is the formulation of words and ideas that define our faithful relationships with God and God's creatures. Therefore, questions about how to think of God and decisions about beliefs in the Holy One are part of womenviews of ethics. Nevertheless, no effort is made here to work out a comprehensive theological position. The emphasis is on only some of the many facets of our experiences of and relationships with God. My conversations with women highlight aspects of God that rarely are emphasized in the male-defined Christian traditions but which womenviews show to be important for faithful Christian life.

An Alternative Approach to Ethics

I arrived at the approach to ethics that is presented in this book for both practical and theological reasons. As I began to teach, I recognized three barriers to student interest in Christian ethics. First was the belief that Christian ideas were handed down from God or the church and were a fait accompli. Students had little or no understanding that divinely inspired men and women had and continue to have the creative ability to image in the signs and symbols, metaphors and visions of their own time and place the experience of a living and active God in human lives and historical events. So I tried to illustrate the human creativity that gave, and continues to give, birth to the Christian moral tradition.

Students also had little if any visionary insight, and this made teaching Christian ethics in relation to current issues almost impossible. The students tended to think that the way things are is the way they must be; or they believed that they had two or three options, cast in stone, from which to choose. For example, any criticism of capitalism's exploitation was countered with claims about communism's oppression. Most students seemed unaware that society's choices may not be limited to these two time-weary systems. My second task as a teacher, then, was to unlock the human creativity in the students themselves, so the class could think together about God's actions with and through us in the present.

The most important lesson I have learned by teaching ethics, however, is that reason alone is ineffective. By trial and error I have discovered that unless students' passions are evoked first — their anger or fear or empathy or even disgust — then ethical reasoning is irrelevant and moral action is unimportant to them. To counteract this, I discovered that fertile ground for ethical reflection and moral response was cultivated by stories of my episodes as a public health nurse; or accounts of experiences by some class members; or news items, videos, and field trips that have emotional impact on students. Only in retrospect have I come to realize that my own interest in Christian ethics and my desire to attain the Ph.D. in ethics arose in the context of dealing with emotionally troubling social issues in my day-to-day work in public health. I needed to understand. I needed to know how to act. Students and church members are no different. Passionate concern precedes ethical reflection and action for all of us.

Such experiences with classes of undergraduate and seminary students have brought me to the realization that ethics is an art wrought with passion and reason. This art of ethics is not limited to the interactions of classrooms or the solitary musings of remote scholars. Neither does it come only out of the pastor's study or a special task force of the church. All of God's people are called to be ethical artists who respond to the pains and fears, hopes and dreams — the passions — of our lives by imaging in words and actions ways to dwell in community with one another and God in our time and place. The moral art we create as people of God is not universal or timeless. We do watercolors rather than marble carvings — ethics always is temporary, designed for particular historical moments that evoke our passions, and necessarily related to clearly defined social locations. The art of ethics requires that we humans join together again and again to reimage God and our relationship with God and one another.

A basic shift in theological orientation, however, has influenced my ethical thinking more radically. This shift has more to do with our relationship with God, our experience of the Holy One, than with our ways of thinking about God's nature. I realize in retrospect that when I began to teach I placed a heavy emphasis on logical consistency and appealed frequently to a divinely ordained moral design that was almost determinative. Thus, in thinking ethically about mothers on welfare, I would see the analogy between widows and the fatherless in the Hebrew codes and Prophets, consider their calls for justice a divine command to live within God's moral law, and then logically move to the conclusion that, therefore, we are required to be just and merciful to these mothers and their children. In my moral thinking, then, creative freedom was constrained by law and logic, by prescription and balanced reason; and the relationship was one of obedience to a holy Other.

Gradually my ethical thinking has shifted toward an interactional view. This means that I see the prophetic commands regarding widows and orphans in the context of my own experiences as a public health nurse with the marginalized and oppressed of our world. Just as God is known experientially rather than abstractly, so God's morality is discovered in interactions between and among persons. In other words, we can know God and God's morality because of God's presence with us. God's moral requirements are derived as much from passion as from reason, more often through loving interactions than through law and logic. Thus an interactional view of ethics means that I do not serve the neighbor in need because of the dictates or moral design of a distant God who has given me the gift of reason; but rather God is known and served *in and with* the neighbor.

I could not have made this leap of faith-understanding without the insights derived from women's theological and ethical writings. Because my locations for Christian ethical reflections in this book are my own life experiences, which include many years as a public health nurse serving largely poor women of color and their children, third-world women's Christian writings have been especially helpful. (I am using the term "third-world women," as used by the women themselves, to designate the oppressed women in every nation. "Third-world" refers to "people whose humanity is being denied" regardless of their geographical location.)[1] Third-world women's perspectives have enabled me to bridge theologically and ethically the distance between my own white, middle-class situation in life and the realities of the life circumstances of those I served. From third-world women I have learned in wholly fresh ways about God incarnate, God whose presence is known when we interact with the least powerful and most needy among us.

Thus passion and reason have brought me to the understandings of theology and ethics that I now hold. The pain and anger I felt in my public health nursing have led me to the theological and ethical reconstructions of this book. I write theology and ethics in order to interpret some of my life experiences in faith perspectives.

Combining passion and reason in theology and ethics certainly is not my invention. Beverly Wildung Harrison's poignant and persuasive 1980 address, "The Power of Anger in the Work of Love," has become a classic in women's ethics in one decade.[2] Bärbel von Wartenberg-Potter asserts that anger is "the very heart of theology." She uses the word "anger" intentionally. Even though empathy or compassion might serve some people, for her "these do not yet have within them any power that will lead to change." She goes on to state: "So this is how I declare my point of view, the position I have reached experientially and theoretically: theology — in my case at least — arises out of a concerned heart, and not, as they [scholars and teachers] used to 'con' me, out of a cool head — *sine ira et studio*, without anger and ardour."[3] I agree that intense feelings are needed for Christian theology — articulating our beliefs about God. The same must be said of Christian ethics — articulating a faithful relationship with God and one another. Yet as Wartenberg-Potter sees, a passionate approach is in contrast to some of the basic rules of theological and ethical reflection that have been taught through the years and indeed up to the present. Many theologians (and ethicists) "regard what is human and personal as inferior to what is abstract and general." With Wartenberg-Potter, however, I declare that "we, women, will no longer disregard belly and body, our human wholeness."[4]

This embrace of passion is typical of third-world women's liberation theology as well. Because liberation theology always has as much to do with the practice of faith as the object of faith, most third-world women's theology also is ethics. Korean women doing theology (and ethics) with and for oppressed, exploited, and alienated women refuse to adopt "a neutral, detached, objective reason." Instead, they call for engagement, taking sides, and passionate involvement.[5] Another way of expressing the place of passion in theology and ethics comes from meetings of Christian women of Africa, Asia, and Latin America. Summarizing these meetings, Virginia Fabella and Mercy Amba Oduyoye say that women "feel called to do scientific theology passionately, . . . a theology made not only with the mind but also with the heart, the body, the womb."[6]

An ethic of passion and reason engages the heart and the head, feelings and ideas, the whole person. It begins with emotionally charged concerns but leads to rational analysis and moral reflection. Passion alone evokes only *reaction* if it is not guided by reason that seeks information, weighs and measures all factors in light of a moral frame of reference, and then chooses appropriate action. Without passion we are not motivated; without reason we are not effective.

The Design of the Book

I have argued that women are imaging Christian theology and ethics in creative ways that reflect uniquely female experiences and perceptions. I also have asserted that Christian ethics is an art wrought with passion and reason. The design of this book mirrors and integrates these presuppositions in several ways.

In part 1, the art of ethics is emphasized. Each chapter begins with an autobiographical sketch that evokes an artistic metaphor for thinking ethically. These metaphors then take on particular meanings for author and reader as understandings of being human are worked out in dialogue with diverse womenviews, derived from women's lived realities. In chapter 2, painting is used as a metaphor for the transcending freedom experienced in human creativity. Cooking, the imagery invoked for chapter 3, provides a creative way of speaking about human dependency, experienced daily in our need for food and other life-supports. Quilting functions in chapter 4 as a creative way to think about cooperation — about working with one another and with God toward common goals for just and merciful human life. Weaving is the artistic image employed in chapter 5, where insights from the three previous chapters are interwoven to reveal alternative understandings of power. Out of the stories, metaphors, and dialogues emerges a way of thinking ethically about Christian life in today's world.

The need for both passion and reason in the art of ethics is more systematically expressed in part 2. Here each chapter begins with a narrative that tells about one of my pain-filled experiences in public health nursing. The remembered pain leads to critical analyses of societal factors that contribute to the social crises to be considered: mothers on welfare, women facing reproductive choices, and persons with addictions, handicapping conditions, or catastrophic diseases. Then the moral norms of part 1 serve as mirrors in which to view the social crises ethically. Suggestions for impassioned and reasoned action follow from this ethical reflection.

PART ONE

Christian Womenviews
of Being Human

2

PAINTING

The Transcending Experience of Creativity

Painting

The sky literally danced with clouds, like happy children freed from school for the day, dizzily singing and twirling and running through an open field. A moment later I realized that the clouds seemed to be fleeing not a day of captivity, but of danger. An ominous mood lurked behind the swiftly and erratically changing sky. A storm was approaching. I was returning from a shopping trip, driving my dilapidated old car to our home overlooking not only the lower Chesapeake Bay to the east but the horizon on all sides — the sweep of the waves, beach, and dunes to the north and south, the marsh and struggling, straggly pines to the west. I deeply inhaled the salt air and sensed the temperature drop as an onshore breeze relieved the heat of another sultry fall day in Virginia. Visible now with the wide expanse of the marsh, a dying pine tree, spotlighted by low sunlight, stood in stark defiance against its own creeping demise and the threatening deep purple sky. The golden cast of late afternoon shimmered on the wheat-colored marsh grasses.

This fleeting moment that filled me to the brim and overflowed stirred up in me the creative urges of the artist. As I completed the short trip home I etched the tree in my mind and chose the pigments needed to capture the colors of the vistas. I mentally arranged the sky and the tree and the marsh — all seen from different and moving perspectives — into the rectangular shape of the watercolor paper. By the time I turned into the driveway, I had anticipated the technique I would use to capture and yet not freeze the movement of the clouds. Unlike the photographer, the painter can create anew out of the given created order. Unlike the person painting with oils or acrylics, the watercolorist can hazard to use water, paper, and pigment to image movement.

As soon as the children were bathed and in bed I filled the tub with water and began soaking the paper. It had to be as wet as I could get it — always a problem in a household with one tub. The colors had to explode into the wet paper in order to portray the sense of near chaos of clouds

11

racing across the sky before an oncoming storm. Yet in this very technique the artist lost control.

The next morning, I watched almost prayerfully, with expectation but also with fear, to see what the pigment and water would do as my trembling hand moved the color-filled brush across wet white paper and ventured to transform it into something not only different from itself but different from the mental picture. I wanted to capture the mood of that sky, the sensuousness of those brief moments on the drive home that I had to convey to others through my painting. Somehow, this artistic talent released the spiritual in the mundane and revealed life in the awe-full power of the storm, the glowing decay of the tree, and the lingering sunlight on the dying marsh grasses.

My artistic endeavors have been life-giving. Yet because of dominant views of human creativity and transcendence, for most of my life I have seen artwork as something we humans do with our minds and our hands to rise above the realities of life. Despite the need for manual skills and tools, in my painting I believed that I transcended the corporeality and materiality of human existence. Womenviews of creativity and transcendence have provided different vistas that have inspired me to paint whole new understandings of our human creativity and our abilities to transcend those aspects of our lives that make us less than human.

Images of Creativity

In a studio displaying works of Japanese women artists hangs a painting by Tomiyama Daeko. She has depicted the scene from Isaiah (11:6–9) where babies play with wild beasts, lambs and kids lie down with wolves and lions, plants are lush and abundant. At the center of this vision of life in relationship with God is a house in which a woman is giving birth to a child.[1] By imaging God's empowering presence with us as a woman in childbirth, the artist has painted a different portrait not only of God but also of women. She has rendered holy what Asian culture denigrates in patriarchal marriages, prostitution, rape for control, and murder for social power.[2]

An American feminist also images God as mother. "God as the giver of life, as the power of being in all being, can be imaged through the metaphor of mother," writes Sallie McFague. The love that gives birth to new life "nurtures what it has brought into existence, wanting growth and fulfillment for all."[3] McFague adds, however, that one can be parental in ways that are not biological, and her imaging of God as mother rests precisely on a larger understanding than giving birth to a child or even being an adoptive parent. "All human beings have the potential for passing life along, for helping to bring the next generation (of whatever kind of beings) into existence, nurturing and guiding it, and working toward its fulfillment." She suggests just a few examples, such as "teaching, medicine, gardening, and social work," and then enlarges the idea to include "almost any cultural, political, economic, or social activity" that fosters and nurtures life.[4]

The image of mother was drawn in larger than parental dimensions by a woman who was active in the revolution of Nicaragua. Shortly before her death, she wrote to her daughter: " 'Mother' does not mean being the woman who gives birth to and cares for a child; to be a mother is to feel in your own flesh the suffering of all the children, all the men, and all the young people who die, as though they had come from your own womb." Her letter conveys the message that "mother" is the one who cares about the kind of world in which all live, who understands her God-given gifts of creativity to be more than biological, to be political, economic, and social. A woman's calling is to create a world where she can "smile for joy, see our people growing like happy children, see them become the new person, honest and conscious of their responsibilities to all humankind."[5]

Mercy Amba Oduyoye also portrays women's creativity in larger than reproductive dimensions. Reflecting on the creation hymn in Genesis 1, she asserts that women, too, are "active beings cooperating with God in the business of creation." Women are "creative, caring creatures, who, after the image of God, conquer chaos to bring forth good out of a nebulous existence."[6]

These women of Asia, the Americas, and Africa paint both God and humankind in relation to women's particular female contexts of creativity. On the one hand, women's reproductive experiences enable them to see that both God's creativity and women's creativity are related to life; and God's creative activities in this world can be understood as embodied rather than spiritual, relational and concerned rather than distant and disinterested. On the other hand, God's creativity enables women to see that their creativity is not restricted to biological parenting; it is perceived as divine calling to create a life-affirming earth. Because of women's biological uniqueness and culturally defined roles as nurturers, they know that to be created in the image of the Creating One is to do more than bring forth new humankind. Women are given the power to create a world that is safe and good for human life. Just as God created an environment to support plant, animal, and human life, women know that as creators of new life they also are creators of a world that nurtures life.

Throughout the global village, women are painting God in new images as they come to understand themselves to be created in God's image. This reimaging of God in turn provides new images for human life. These womenviews are important additions to the Christian traditions, which have been based on erroneous and limited views of human life. Many factors have led to the errors and limitations, but two that are of central importance are not always recognized.

First, the Bible and most of the writings that make up the Christian traditions were written when the dominant culture held to an agricultural view of human reproduction that seems completely ludicrous to late twentieth-century minds. People of the Mediterranean basin believed — following a rationale worked out explicitly by Aristotle in the fourth century BCE — that the male was the sole creator of new life. The man's body produced a limited number of tiny replicas of himself that he planted one by one in the woman's womb, where the seed would grow to be a male (a normal human being) in a fertile womb but a female (an abnormal being) in a womb that was not hospitable and healthy. This was the culture's way to explain the birth of a female child, needed because the seed that was planted was believed to be a miniature male. The idea is analogous to the planting of vegetable seeds in soil needing water and fertilizer or in places without adequate sun; in such conditions robust plants and fruits like those from which the seeds were taken do not grow.

Such a truncated agricultural understanding of human reproduction shaped Christian understandings of God and human life. Alternative theories of reproduction, suggesting a larger role for women, were operative in the culture. Nevertheless, the view that only men produced the seeds of reproduction, with slight modifications, was upheld by the male-dominated scientific community until the nineteenth century and, due to widespread resistance, in Western society generally until the second decade of this century. According to a Presbyterian Church (U.S.A.) study, although present understandings of reproductive science were accepted in veterinary medicine earlier, it was not until 1875 that the German embryologist Karl Ernest von Baer theorized that human reproduction also results from the combination of egg and sperm. Neither the medical profession nor the church was ready to accept his views until after the First World War.[7] Instead, in an era of both Darwinian and feminist challenges, agricultural views of human reproduction were maintained. In the context of such understandings of human reproduction, biblical interpretations and theological constructions have based ideas about God and humanity on the beliefs that only males are fully human, and only men are creators of new life and imagers of God, the creating One. These views in turn have led to thinking of God as male.

A second and equally distorting factor in Christian views of God and human life comes from the fact that with rare and largely ignored exceptions, until the last two decades theology was formulated by men. Because of their relatively minor biological role in human reproduction and their culturally defined roles that take them away from child rearing, men can separate themselves physically from the processes of birth and nurture. This reality, combined with the denigration of the body and things earthly in the Western culture in which Christianity arose and developed, led to disembodied and unrealistic views of human life. This in turn influenced the ways God was described. In contrast, many women's theologies and ethics criticize and attempt to overcome the problems of Western dualism, which separates life into mental and physical or spiritual and bodily spheres. Embodiment has become a major corrective premise in feminist theology and ethics, as seen in the work of Beverly Wildung Harrison, who speaks of "our bodies, ourselves" as a way of overcoming dualism.[8]

Theology is the articulation of our experiences of God's presence in our lives. As human beings we cannot get outside of our bodies or our culture when we try to find ways to image this God whom we experience in creating and nurturing ways. If our understandings of human life are flawed and limited, we cannot but have flaws and limitations in our views of God, in whose image we are created. Conversely, if our views of God are flawed or distorted, we cannot but have flaws and distortions in our understandings of human life.

Womenviews are enlarging Christian understandings of both divine and human creativity. For women, creating new life is an embodied reality that lasts physically for many years and emotionally for their lifetimes. Thus womenviews of the creating God, in whose image women and men are made, are rooted in the concrete realities of human existence. For most women, these concrete realities have to do not only with creating and nurturing new life, but also with providing a habitat that affirms and sustains life. A God who creates humankind in God's image must be conceptualized in terms of both male and female experiences. Women's experiences, be they biological or cultural, provide needed alternative perspectives to complement the lopsided menviews that are so prevalent in Christian faith.

Womenviews of Transcending Creativity

The different roles men and women play in creating human life — and these roles are dissimilar physically even in today's world where social roles are changing — may make it impossible for men and women to have the same understandings of God and humanity. As already suggested, perhaps men's tendency to separate themselves physically from the day-to-day activities of human reproduction, nurturing, and related life-sustaining processes explains why men have thought of God and human life in terms of world-escaping transcendence. Reinhold Niebuhr's classic work, *The Nature and Destiny of Man*,[9] reflected this male view. Niebuhr believed that the Genesis 1 creation hymn shows that God is transcendent, free of the creation and its creatures. Thus to be created in this God's image is to be self-transcendent, able to stand outside of or rise above ourselves and see ourselves objectively as creatures with Godlike qualities. For Niebuhr, this transcendence is the essence of human freedom and together with our finitude inevitably leads to human sin.

Niebuhr's views of divine and human transcendence, which reflected the neo-orthodoxy that has influenced Christian theology for the past fifty years, are incongruent to women who draw on experiences of childbearing and parenting to do theology. As seen already, for women the belief that they too are created in God's image and are therefore creators gives them the freedom to be artists of their world, designers of life and life-supporting structures. This creativity is an embodied freedom. Women's embodied views enable them to think in female ways about God's and humanity's transcending creativity.

Sallie McFague, who images God as mother, points out that the creation stories have been interpreted as depicting intellectual, aesthetic acts of God, like the work of a disinterested, dispassionate, and separated artisan. "But the model of God as mother suggests a very different kind of creation."[10] In this chapter, which is built around the metaphor of painting, I see human creativity as a single piece and not as something separated into artistic and birthing processes. Therefore, a problem arises for me in McFague's two kinds of creativity. My own intellectual journey forces me to agree with McFague that traditionally the creation stories have been interpreted in ways that radically separate Creator and creation; but she sees a dichotomy between the creativity of an artist and that of a mother that in retrospect my own experiences as both artist and mother do not bear out. Indeed, the two were so similar to me that I could not do them both at the same time; when I was pregnant and lactating, my artwork was put away. In my experience, everything that is created takes its life and its image from its creator — be it painting or a child. For me, the pain and joy of the creative processes of the artist are different from the birthing and parenting processes in *degree* but not in *kind*.

Nevertheless, McFague's imaging of God as a birthing mother mirrors God's transcending creation of our world "as a physical event: the universe is bodied forth from God, it is expressive of God's very being." Imagery such as this conveys the idea that "the universe and God are neither totally distant nor totally different." Instead, "they are close and similar," just as "a mother and her child have a sense of affinity and kinship."[11] Such use of birth imagery is a radical challenge to the idea of a God who is transcendent and wholly other than the creation. Women know that the life to which they give birth is part of them and they are part of it.

Women need not draw on experiences of birth and parenthood to derive alternatives to traditional male, European-American views of a transcendent and wholly other God. Very diverse life experiences also help women to paint God's transcending creativity with colors that differ from prevailing menviews.

Comparing creation myths of prepatriarchal and patriarchal societies, Nelle Morton saw that in patriarchal religion, the spirit was separated from the body, torn from its organic origins in mother, earth, and goddess. With the advent of patriarchal religions, "the moving verb *transcending* (synonymous with breath and spirit) changed to a static noun, *transcendence,* separated from the body and woman." For Morton, a foresister of the American feminist movement of the 1960s, such patriarchal views led to the understanding of God's transcendence that now dominates Christianity. In the hierarchical worldview of patriarchy and Christianity, the Spirit is understood to descend from its transcendence above life, and this descending Spirit suggests power over. By contrast, in the organic worldview of prepatriarchal goddess religions, the transcending spirit of breath and life rises, and this ascending spirit suggests the power of life out of the heart of the people.[12]

Carter Heyward, American feminist-liberationist, provides another alternative to the dominant view of God and humans as transcendent in a hierarchical and disembodied sense. "To transcend means, literally, to cross over. To bridge. To make connections. To burst free of particular locations," says Heyward. Heyward regrets that we have spent so many years seeing God's immanence as an aspect of God that we experience and God's transcendence as an aspect of God that is mystery, outside our experience, the "God beyond God." She believes many Christians are experiencing a "wonderfully mysterious power truly crossing over into and through and from our lives into the lives of all created beings — and that this power is indeed God, transcendent precisely in the fullness and radicality of her immanence among us."[13]

Combining the many insights of diverse women leads to the conclusion that God is not free *from* human life but free *for and in* human life, freely involved in the creation and with the human creatures brought forth in the pains of labor. If God is among us, freely and creatively transcending the barriers to our divinely ordained life — barriers that cause suffering to us and to God, who is like a loving mother — then we who are created in God's image are to do the same. To be created in the image of creating and transcending God is to be free to create a life that transcends barriers to our full humanity. To be created in God's image means to be creatures whose roles are to create not only life but also a life-nurturing world.

Creativity as Moral Endeavor

Images of birth and nurture encourage a rethinking of the experiences and purposes of all human creativity. Womenviews of transcending creativity invite reinterpretations of human freedom. Both lead to distinctly moral ways of understanding Christian life.

Women's images of female and divine birthing and nurturing activities do not reduce creativity to the reproduction and sustenance of our species. The creative work of artists and inventors, and the cultural and technological artifacts they produce, are not excluded in such a view of creativity. Neither does this view overlook the creative reconstructing of science, law, philosophy, religion, government, business, or human relationships and communities of every kind. Nevertheless, by framing divine and human creativity in birth and nurturing images, a moral norm that creativity of any kind must foster and sustain life is established.

The reality of our existence, however, is that much human creativity has not been devoted to purposes of giving and supporting life. As Judith Groch has seen, "the creative process which produces a sword is the same as that which results in a scalpel; that which synthesizes a new medicine is no different from the one which yields a poison."[14] Our ability to transcend natural and social situations by creating different circumstances does not always lead to results that image the creating and transcending God who has been painted from womenviews.

In my lifetime, two of the most concerted creative efforts of American society have been the Manhattan Project, which gave birth to the atomic bomb,[15] and the Apollo program, which propelled American astronauts to the moon. There are marked similarities and dissimilarities in the two efforts, however. Both embodied transcending creativity in that new creations enabled humans to cross natural barriers. Both employed some of the greatest minds of our nation, and, as they were further developed, both required disproportionate financial resources. Thus talent and money were siphoned away from other needs of humanity and our earthly habitat.

The differences are just as important. On the one hand, the Manhattan Project led to the bombing of Hiroshima and Nagasaki, widespread radiation contamination of people and land, and a world that has lived for decades on the brink of self-annihilation. On the other hand, anyone whose life or health has been saved by nuclear analysis of blood or magnetic resonance imaging sees the aftermath of this human achievement as life-giving rather than life-threatening. Nuclear energy is more ambiguous; it may create as many problems as it solves. And all nuclear technology generates hazardous wastes that could haunt the planet for aeons.

Most people see the space race in more unambiguously positive terms, but are there grounds for that positive assessment? On the one hand, space technology has yielded enormous gains for earthly life, from cookware to communications, and so much more. On the other hand, fueled in part by the "Star Trek" television series and movies, space travel has taken on religious connotations. Many in the generation that was born in the 1950s and 1960s have seen space as not only the last frontier but also the only hope for saving a remnant of the human race. Convinced that we would destroy habitat earth, these people have come to believe that space offers the only escape.

These two examples illustrate the reality that our transcending creativity can be employed for what may seem to be life-protecting or enhancing purposes and turn out to have life-threatening or denying consequences. Our innovative and barrier-crossing abilities pose difficult moral challenges because we cannot foresee the future. Yet a norm of fostering and nurturing life provides a standard by which we can try to assess and guide our transcending creativity. If life is our goal, it also can be a measure that enables us to direct creative talent and energy and our financial resources toward only that which we believe will be life-engendering work. Imagine what our life might be if the same degree of creativity and resources that went into the Manhattan Project and the nuclear arms race, or the Apollo program and the space race, had been directed toward education, economic growth that makes jobs, and affordable and available health services for all (to name just a few areas needing such efforts). Picture a world without the ever-present nuclear threat or the hazardous wastes generated by unchecked nuclear technology. Envision a society just as devoted to a healthy, life-supporting habitat earth as to space exploration.

The views of transcending creativity set forth above also challenge conventional ways of thinking about human freedom. In Western culture, human freedom has been thought of religiously and philosophically as the ability to transcend our embodiment in spiritual or mental ways; and it has been understood socially or politically as independence. In both cases, freedom has been cast in terms of freedom *from* something that is seen negatively. Clearly there are individuals, communities, and governments who behave in ways that impede human freedom to creatively transcend barriers that interfere with fully human life. For most of human history men have restricted women and children. Many communities have customs and mores that are narrowly defined so that anyone who hears a different drummer is ostracized or marginalized. And some governments are socially and economically so oppressive that many if not most of the people under them are reduced to less than human status. All people do need to be free *from* these impediments to life. But freedom *from* interference or oppression does not necessarily translate to freedom *for* fully human life. This will become even more apparent as the chapters that follow are read. For the present, a redefinition of freedom is needed. What is it? How is it experienced? Is exercising it morally binding for human life?

Letty Russell argued in her ground-breaking 1974 book that women and other oppressed peoples need freedom from internal and external restraints in order to serve. She claimed that for Christians freedom *from* oppression is for the purpose of having freedom *for* servanthood.[16] Much of Russell's work over the past two decades has continued this theme in various keys. She has emphasized human partnership with God and one another to serve our world. What I am proposing in this book agrees as a whole with Russell's basic premise about human freedom. Reinterpreting freedom in the context of womenviews of transcending creativity, however, leads to additional insights.

To be created in God's image as a creating and transcending being is to be given the freedom for self-determination. Such freedom does not mean independence — it cannot be exercised without both the help and cooperation of other humans and God's gracious empowerment. The freedom experienced and exercised in transcending creativity is the God-given ability to make choices, to survive the natural orders that threaten life, to be more than our biology. When we have the freedom to be creators of our world and to transcend barriers to fully human life, our destinies are not determined by birth or fate or the stars or the gods or even our God. We are not flotsam and jetsam in the ebb and flow of life. Even though we cannot totally control our world, we can design rudders and erect sails that enable us to choose directions and courses of actions for our lives, individually and corporately.

Ultimately our freedom to create and transcend is God's gift for survival. Survival is not an idea readily accepted in Christian theology, which has emphasized sacrifice; yet the power to survive is inherent in our power to create and sustain life — a power we share with all God's creatures. As I have etched the ideas of this chapter, my husband and I have been taught a lesson about the lowly rodent's transcending creativity for survival. A squirrel who inhabits our yard is determined to get into the bird feeders. Here we are, two highly educated people with finely honed manual skills, yet we are repeatedly outsmarted by the squirrel who is hungry. We try a new way to baffle this persistent squirrel only to watch it sit on a tree, observe the situation, and then after one or more tries perch securely in one of the feeders and happily gobble up the birdseed. Without transcending creativity, God's creatures — all of us — could not devise shelters and clothing, or find food, or store and preserve food. Our freedom, then, is freedom to survive.

For fully human life, however, our survival depends on more than existence. Persons do need food and shelter and other life necessities; but as imagers of God we also are creators of life and life circumstances that allow us to change our world so that human personalities and relationships can flourish. Thus human freedom seen in the light of transcending creativity has everything to do with the moral imperative of life. To be fully alive we must be free to create life in its largest dimensions and to transcend barriers to full participation in our common life. Freedom, then, is as much a moral imperative as life. The creation and sustenance of life guide us in the ways we exercise our freedom. At the same time, freedom is morally necessary in order that we can be imagers of our God who through us continues to create and sustain human life in all of its multiple dimensions.

Christian womenviews, then, lead to the belief that our freedom to be creative — in whatever art or human endeavor — is directly related to what it means to be faithful, to image the One who is freely creating life and transcending barriers to life. As creators of life and life-sustaining circumstances, women can understand that because all humans are created in the image of the creating and transcending God, all of us must be free to bring order out of chaos so that an environment supportive of life can be maintained. Such an environment fosters the creation of new life, by which women mean more than reproduction of species. An environment that nurtures creativity provides the power and hope of transcending barriers to life-affirming situations, of creating new life in societal institutions as well as in human hearts and minds and bodies.

3

COOKING
The Radical Reality of Dependence

Cooking

My world had closed in on me. Instead of soaking up four horizons in a light-filled house, I resided in a town house facing east and west, nestled in a crowd of buildings under lofty loblolly pines that defied the sun summer and winter and discouraged every attempt to create an atmosphere of light and openness. I was now a single head of household with a daughter in college and two teenage sons; emotional and economic survival, rather than watercolor renditions of breathtaking vistas, was the stuff of my existence. I had given up the freedom of movement and creative nursing of fieldwork in public health, my vocation for the previous five years, and accepted a transfer to clinical duty. I had difficulty adjusting to day after day in a clinic with no windows after years spent out in the city, traveling in the car from place to place on my rounds to patients and families who were homebound. I felt pain as I changed from self-directed work to a clearly defined routine under the direction of a doctor. As a single parent it was a sacrifice I chose, however, because I wanted to be available by phone for my children, and I wanted to be in a safer environment.

When I pulled into the parking lot at the end of one workday, my seventeen-year-old son ran from the house, growled something about my being late *again,* and jumped into the car to go to work. He had chosen to work part-time bussing tables rather than see me take on a second job. Our schedules meshed well for a while, but lately the clinic had been so busy that it was impossible for me to get away on time. I understood his anger, but it hurt. I was grateful that he was willing to help support us, that we could depend on him; but I grieved at the cost to him.

Opening the door, I heard my younger son call, "Hey mom, what's for supper?" "Whatever you want to fix, because I'm too tired to care," I responded, shedding my uniform as I headed for the shower. A few minutes later I felt human again. The smell of supper cooking stimulated my appetite, and I joined my son for hot dogs, french fries, and canned corn; none of these is my favorite food (the combination appealed to neither my palate nor my nutritional insights), and yet I was thankful for a son on whom I could depend for basic necessities, and I shared his food offering with pleasure.

Five years later, I returned to fieldwork in public health nursing. I had moved to a new apartment with more light and view. With all three children out of the home, I was finishing my baccalaureate degree part-time and boldly designing and implementing programs with churches in a two hundred–mile radius. At last, I had regained my sense of creative freedom, and I was healed. Yet my weekends were so full due to church meetings or library research for term papers that my daughter, concerned for her mother's health, took it upon herself to visit frequently in order to shop and cook. Once again I found my life enriched because I could depend on one of my children for basic needs.

Our need for sustenance and for one another come together for me in these memories. We often think that children are dependent on parents, and indeed this is the case from conception to age two or three. Yet from the time my children could talk and understand what was happening, I have been able to depend on them when I was sick, tired, hurt, or hungry. This kind of parent-child relationship fosters a healthy respect for dependence that is not only the reality of our finitude but also can be understood creatively when related to cooking — an art of preparing food for human survival and community.

My own acceptance of dependence as inherent in our humanity was many years in the making. Only after I read and heard and talked with women who are calling into question independence for philosophical, theological, and ethical reasons, moreover, did I begin to glean that in dependence can be found insights about not only ourselves but also God. Diverse womenviews, then, have served as recipes to enable me to move step-by-step through first embracing my own dependence, then recognizing God's dependence, and finally realizing the necessity of dependence as a moral category for Christians.

Images of Dependence

The Bakossi people of Cameroon classify stones into two groups, living and dead. "Living stones are stones that are movable, portable and usable."[1] For Bakossi women, the living stones that have the greatest significance are the tripod stones used for cooking. "These stones serve a vital purpose in the life of the family and the community," says Grace Eneme. "Around them people meet for family discussions. Here is where moral instruction takes place and folk tales are told, a place of warmth and a refuge for strangers."[2] Eneme's story about the customs of her African people illustrates that cooking evokes images not only of our need for nutrition, but also of our need for one another in social and cultural ways. Thus cooking is an image that reveals the depths of our dependence on the necessities of life and one another.

These same needs are central to Christian traditions, but cooking and feeding images are subordinated and ignored by Christians, or spiritualized and theologized to the extent that bodily dependence on food is no longer recognized. This trend in Christianity reflects our culture, which thinks in terms of independence rather than dependence. Indeed, in today's world "dependent" and "dependence" are words used in derogatory ways to negate the worth or health of persons or groups. A welfare mother's dependence on the state is decried, and the afflictions of addiction are labeled "dependence" (and "co-dependence"). Peoples of the Southern Hemisphere, on whom nations of the Northern Hemisphere have been dependent for economic growth, are now seen negatively because they are dependent on foreign aid. The connotation is that dependence renders persons less than fully human and nations less valuable. Dependence is seen as the opposite of healthy humanity, when in fact it is the root reality of being human.

Christians, along with the rest of society, buy into the myth of independence and deny the reality of dependence. Thus we hear Jesus' words "one does not live by bread alone" (Luke 3:4b) rather than Christ's cry of pain and sorrow in "for I was hungry and you gave me no food, I was thirsty and you gave me nothing to drink" (Matt. 25:42). In the feeding stories, we hear the miracle rather than Jesus' concern for the hunger of the people: "Where are we to buy bread for these people to eat?" (John 6:5b). In the postresurrection account of John (21:1–13), we hear the miracle of the huge fish catch rather than the disciples' need for a livelihood; and we find numerous theological ways to explain away the meal prepared for the disciples who will be hungry after their work. Our very sacrament of the Eucharist — originally part of a hearty meal, a feast — is a fast, a mere taste of bread and wine. It is no longer a nourishing meal to feed hungry co-workers.

If the stories of Jesus feeding the people and the disciples were connected to our utter dependence on food, how differently we would understand Christianity, our God, and ourselves. Jesus showed us in his concern about our need for food that God cares about the basic necessities of our lives. In other words, Jesus showed that God loves and accepts us precisely at the point of our dependence on the creation and one another. Both creation stories say that humans are created in the context of the vegetation that is needed to support animal and human life. Of course, scientific evidence has proved that the oxygen provided by plant life makes the earth hospitable for animal and human life. Yet from the beginning of the Hebrew-Christian tradition, long before there was scientific knowledge about the source of or even the need for oxygen, people understood God as the one who provided plants for life. Thus scripture teaches that God creates beings whose very lives depend on bodily necessities.

Our sexuality and need for companionship also are ways in which God creates us to be dependent on the natural order and one another. In Genesis 1, our creation as male and female is immediately followed by the directive to be sexually interdependent in order to complete God's work of creation. In Genesis 2, the division of the earth creature into male and female is done because God knows that the earth creature needs a helper to tend God's creation, and the Hebrew word used here for helper is the same one used later to describe God as the helper of the people of Israel.[3] Both stories indicate that humans need humans: humans are dependent on other humans as well as on God and the earth habitat God has made.

Our need for the earth and all its resources is graphically portrayed by Elizabeth Dodson Gray, who argues that "we exist on this planet not in dominion, but like fetuses. We are totally dependent on this planet for all the functions essential to our living." As she explains, the biosphere of habitat earth provides our air, food, and water, and disposes of our wastes just as the placenta does these things for the unborn in its mother's body.[4] Gray's imagery reaches down into the recesses of our very existence to emphasize the fundamental nature of our dependence on the habitat we call earth. Her images of human nourishment in the reproductive processes powerfully express the reality and radicality of humanity's dependence.

Despite ancient and contemporary theological foundations that might lead to different understandings, Christianity has done little to transcend the cultural emphasis on independence, the "self-made" woman or man. Most Christians are not ready to admit that life is experienced in terms of fundamental dependence on one another. Yet dependence is a universal experience of every one of us, even if we try to deny or ignore it. Thus it should be addressed theologically and ethically.

Womenviews of Human and Divine Dependence

Increasingly women are calling into question our culture's belief in and search for untethered freedom and independence. Women's questioning of *independence* as a way of life to be sought can be instructive and implicitly issues an invitation for new thinking about *dependence*.

Speaking about relationship as a feminist moral category, Beverly Wildung Harrison insists on "the deep, total sociality of all things. All things cohere in each other. Nothing living is self-contained; if there were such a thing as an unrelated individual, none of us would know it." Harrison goes on to argue that "our life is part of a vast cosmic web, and no moral theology that fails to envisage reality in this way will be able to make sense of our lives or our actions today."[5]

Neither human finitude nor the limits placed on us by nature can be controlled or escaped, asserts Sharon Welch. "They can, however, be endured and survived. It is possible for there to be a dance with life, a creative response to its intrinsic limits and challenges."[6] Welch shows that in *The Courage to Be*,[7] Paul Tillich, who articulated the European and male views that dominated mid–twentieth-century America, interpreted human interdependence as threatening. Yet Welch writes that "in poetry, prose, and philosophy, feminists are celebrating another possibility, the acknowledgement of contingency, our belonging to the web of life, as a complex, challenging, and wondrous gift."[8]

Even as women offer alternatives to independence, dependence is not an idea that most want to embrace. Women, who have been rendered economically and socially dependent on men in this patriarchal society — indeed, expected to find their very identities in their dependence on fathers, husbands, and sons — are understandably fearful of dependence. Despite this reality, Carter Heyward urges women not to fear mutuality, not to try to escape from interrelatedness into a world of separatism and independence.[9]

The preceding womenviews hold up alternatives to the worship of independence. Yet interdependence, connectedness, and mutuality are not sufficient to meet the moral needs of our society. The reality of our existence is that all of us at some time are dependent in ways that are not reciprocal — indeed, often in ways that separate or disconnect us from others; and for reasons beyond our control some of us spend most if not all of our lives in a dependent, rather than interdependent or mutual, state. We need to accept the reality and radicality of dependence on one another as the sine qua non of being human. Therefore, I will use women's mirrors to reimage God in Christ so that theological resources can be gained for an ethical understanding of dependence that meets human needs in our time.

Women's mirrors reflect lived realities that point to theological insights. In the United States, women who work in the home to rear and maintain a family are considered "dependents." This label is applied equally to married women who do not work outside the home and single mothers who receive welfare support, although with different connotations (as will be shown in chapter 6). The label ignores the reality that in most two-parent families the man is at least as dependent on the woman as she is on him; and our social structure and economy would collapse without the voluntary efforts of women and the part-time labor at exploitative wages provided by women who supplement their husband's incomes or their welfare checks. Women, whether they work in the home or in the marketplace or both, know that their husbands and children, aging parents and parents-in-law, as well as our society's communal and economic structures, are dependent on them. The dependence of men, children, and aged parents on women is felt even by professional women who do not marry or have children; extended families expect such women to care for brothers, nieces and nephews, and parents.

Women, on whom men, children, parents, and our whole socioeconomic structure are so dependent, need to lift up dependence as an experience of humanness. Out of this lived reality women can find alternative ways to reconceptualize not only human dependence but God's dependence as well. Once dependence is accepted as the way we all experience being human, then we can enlarge our understanding of its place in human life. We can admit that ultimately our existence is dependent on God, but in reality our existence also is dependent on our parents, most especially our mothers, as well as all the rest of the human race and habitat earth.

Perhaps we never will take seriously our own dependence on God, much less our dependence on neighbors and the earth habitat, until we accept God's dependence on us. We usually are ready to proclaim that we are created in the image of God. Seldom do we ask what that means. In the previous chapter, I argued that it means that we are creators, like the Creating One, and we can transcend — cross over and between and among — like the Transcending One, to bring harmony out of chaos, health out of sickness. But God also is dependent on human creatures, not for God's ultimate existence, but for God's presence and work in the world. Genesis 2 tells of God creating the earth creature to till the garden. In Genesis 1, the creatures of God are given the care of the earth and the role of continuing its creation. God called upon Abraham and Sarah to begin a righteous people and upon Moses to free those people. God called forth the prophets to speak the holy word to the people and Mary to give birth to the Messiah. All of these people on whom God depended for a continuing working relationship with the creatures were free to refuse God's request. In other words, God's work in the world was dependent on their affirmative responses. All of these people who did answer God's call in the affirmative also recognized their dependence on God's transcending and ever-creating presence and guidance.

These realizations, derived from the biblical narratives, prompt probing questions: How is God dependent on us today? and How can a dependent God be a creating and transcending presence for and with us now? These questions require revised understandings of Christ — presented by the church in hymns and prayers, creeds and catechisms, as spiritual Lord and heavenly King, but known in the Gospels as a dependent human being. Women's interpretations invite alternative ways of thinking about Christ; and third-world women's perspectives are most helpful for this task.

A major influence in third-world women's thinking about Christ is the belief expressed in the parable of the last judgment in Matt. 25:31–46: "Just as you did not do it to one of the least of these, you did not do it to me" (45). "This notion of 'the least' is attractive because it descriptively locates the condition of Black women," writes Jacquelyn Grant about the experiences of African-American women. "The least" expresses black women's experiences of a "tri-dimensional reality" of racism, sexism, and classism.[10]

Basing her argument on a similar interpretation of the same biblical passage, Louise Tappa of Cameroon insists that African theology must start and develop in the context of the oppressed situation of African women. Since African women are "at the bottom of the scale," they incarnate Christ in that they are the least powerful and most needy of the people.[11] The perspectives of Thérèsa Souga, also of Cameroon, both embrace and enlarge Tappa's views. Her argument hinges on Jesus' interest in and identity with women. She shows that God is revealed by Jesus most clearly in his connections with women. First, God confounds humans by being born of a woman.[12] Christians need to reflect deeply on this reality. God's presence in human life is manifest in Jesus, thus revealing to us God and also humanity as God intends us to be. Yet like the rest of us this Jesus was born from the womb and suckled at the breasts of a woman; he was utterly dependent. As Souga points out, Jesus revealed God's empowerment among us; but Jesus also chose to identify himself with the powerless, marginalized, and neglected lepers and poor and women and other outcasts of his society, thus giving us in his earthly ministry a foretaste of the Christ who is present in the least powerful and most needy among us. On such a basis, Souga can assert that "Christ is in solidarity with women, for they incarnate the suffering of the African people."[13]

A particular kind of women's sensitivity arises from being among and identifying with the least powerful and most needy among us. Such experiences open María Teresa Porcile of Uruguay to a method of biblical interpretation that she calls "evocation." With artistic imagination, she relates the story of the woman at the well (John 4:1–42) to the situation in a shantytown without water and illustrates poignantly the dependence of Christ-in-the-least-of-these on human response:

> How good it would be to wash his tired feet at least, but where? . . . In the shanty-town there was no water. . . .
> It was evening, and the day had been very hard.
> And Jesus said: "Give me a drink." . . .
>
> The women never left the district now. There they stood at the doors of their huts, surrounded by children, weighed down by the suffocating heat of the day after a sleepless night. . . .
> It was mid-day and the sun was blazing down. . . .
> And Jesus said: "Give me a drink." . . .
>
> A woman passed that way, coming from afar. She was a stranger, someone they didn't know and she carried a bucket. She went up to the well where the children were sitting, and the old people and the men and women, looking at the water in the well — the water, so near and yet so far.

And Jesus said: "Give me a drink."

And the woman answered: "Why do you ask me for a drink? You are poor and I am rich. You are thirsty but the bucket is mine."

And Jesus said: "Woman, what of the well? Whose well is it?" And the woman's eyes were opened and with her bucket they began to draw water for the whole district.[14]

This revealing interpretation, shaped by the context of a Uruguayan shantytown without water, depicts Christ's continuing humanity in and among us, Christ's need for food and water, for a human response to dependence on these necessities of being human. Interpretations such as this and those above reveal in fresh ways Jesus' teaching that Christ is the needy one in the least among us: "I was hungry and you gave me no food, I was thirsty and you gave me nothing to drink" (Matt. 25:42).

Christians are ready and willing to think of Christ as the host at our churches' Communion meals — especially in the more liturgical or eucharistic churches. We need to be as ready and willing to see Christ in the homeless, hungry, and thirsty woman who comes to the soup kitchen: "I was hungry and you gave me food, I was thirsty and you gave me something to drink, I was a stranger and you welcomed me" (Matt. 25:35). Christ will not be present with and for us in the Holy Communion if our church does not have the meal or if we are not present to participate; neither can Christ be present with and for us if we do not recognize the needy Christic presence in the homeless, hungry, and thirsty woman. Indeed, if we do not seek her and meet her needs, she dies and Christ's presence that is manifest in her for us dies with her; and we participate once more in the crucifixion.

Dependence as a Moral Category

Dependence is not a goal of human life but the reality of being human. Yet it is not seen in negative terms if we accept our creatureliness, if we believe that we are created in the image of the One who is needy, the One who depends on us, the One who knows us and is known by us in the least powerful and most needy among us. Such acceptance is part of becoming human.

Even if dependence is accepted as the root reality of being human, however, our dependence is always in tension with the freedom of our transcending and life-affirming creativity. "Our daily dependencies (on nature, our bodies, other selves) are an unavoidable fact of our existence that is itself neutral if not positive," says Mary Potter Engel. Nevertheless, she notes that "we find it hard to reconcile our existence as at once free and dependent."[15] Therefore, many of us experience either "a distortion of the dynamic tension between freedom and dependence, or the lack of consent to the dependence and fragility of our lives." Engel, whose concern is with battered women, says that when a woman is dominated by a man who uses his freedom to abuse, she may choose to abdicate her freedom and become totally dependent in order to survive in the relationship.[16] In such situations, if we choose dependence as a way to escape the difficulties of creating and transcending freedom — even for ourselves — we are refusing our likeness of God's image and distorting dependence as a moral category.

Dependence as a moral category challenges not only independence but some basic tenets of Christian moral traditions. In chapter 1, I stated that my ethics are based on the belief that personal interactions are the loci of moral insight, that passion as much as reason leads to ethical knowledge. In taking this position I am diverging from theories of universal and timeless moral norms that have grown up in Christian moral traditions: natural law, moral order, and biblical codes.

Early Christianity appropriated natural law from Stoicism, a philosophical school in ancient Rome. Christian formulations of natural law achieved their greatest influence in the moral structure of Thomas Aquinas and still dominate Roman Catholic ethics and influence several Protestant denominations. Natural law is the belief that as creatures made in God's image, we participate in our finite and sinful way in the mind of God, the source of eternal law. This gift of God's moral law often is associated with conscience, the individual's way of knowing and choosing moral actions. It is interesting that this Christian belief about human knowledge of good and evil gained its ascendancy in the contest of ideas at the time of the Renaissance (fourteenth to sixteenth centuries), when after years of miserable and self-negating existence, Europeans felt the first flush of pride in their status and declared once again with Pythagoras that "man is the measure of all things." Over the centuries, an increasing belief in human reason has bolstered belief in natural law.

The idea of moral order, another concept of moral design based on creation, arose during the Enlightenment (eighteenth century). It was a time when humans were enamored with their abilities to undertake scientific explorations of the physical order of the universe and rationally explain the regularity of natural laws in physics, biology, and the emerging human and social sciences. Believers in moral order hold that a structure of morality is as much an unchanging and regulating part of the created world as are physical laws such as gravity, and this moral structure can be discovered by scientific methods. Moral order often is defined by analogy to the biochemical order of physiology and ecology. In our freedom we can ignore the restraints of moral order in the short run, just as we can ignore adequate nutrition or fail to respect our earthly environment, only to learn in the final analysis that we have brought doom on ourselves.

Believers in biblical norms and codes as timeless and absolute moral directives base their ethics on convictions that God alone is the source of Hebrew and Christian scriptures. Even though the Bible has been central to Protestantism since the sixteenth century, scientific and cultural challenges to faith over the last century have led to increasingly narrow interpretations by some Christians. Such positions do not allow the error of human judgment or acknowledge the influence of sociocultural factors in the codes of Exodus, Deuteronomy, and Leviticus; further, they do not address the divergence — indeed, contradictions — in the moral teachings of the four Gospels, the writings of Paul and the Pauline community, and the later Catholic Epistles. Prevailing philosophical systems, scientific understandings, and secular social mores at the times of the writings are ignored by many adherents to biblical codes; and yet these cultural factors formed the concepts out of which biblical theology and ethics were articulated.

In arguing that we discern God's morality in the passions of interactions rather than because of divine laws, natural orders, or biblical norms and codes, I am *not* denying a place for reason, science, and the Bible in Christian ethics. We must reflect in a rational way on our experiences of God in human life. Reason and science help us in our moral strategies; we need the information provided by the sciences and scientific methods to implement moral decisions. We can learn from the biblical narratives, letters, and teachings how, in their particular sociocultural contexts, our forebears tried to articulate and live a faithful relationship with God. The Bible teaches us about God so that we understand our own experiences of the creating, transcending, and needing One among us. Insights from philosophical reason, scientific facts, and biblical study can challenge or correct our attempts to do ethics and act morally.

Yet none of these is sufficient for a Christian approach to ethical reflection and moral action. Ours is a faith based on divine-human interaction. Christians believe that God is incarnate in God's world, is Immanuel — God with us. This is a central message of the Gospel writers. As exemplar for human morality, God is known most fully in Jesus of Nazareth and in human-divine-human interactions, in which Christ is in the midst of us. This is explicit in Jesus' teaching, "Just as you did it to one of the least of these who are members of my family, you did it to me" (Matt. 25:40). It is important to remember that "the least of these" are the dispossessed, marginalized, impoverished people, the ones who have the least power and the most need of help from those who can give it. The "least" are not the less valued — indeed, from the Exodus to the resurrection we are assured that the rejected of humanity are the chosen ones of God; they are the most precious and valued among the people. Thus the surest way to know God's moral self "lies in looking at the faces of the women, men, and children who have been entrusted to us, and in whom God, as woman, man, or child, meets us and waits for our response."[17] Christ in the least powerful and most needy among us confronts us with the justice of God, and whether or not we respond with justice and compassion, we know God's expectations.

No doubt, the astute reader already has asked the questions: How do we know God's moral requirements if not by reason or science or biblical codes? How do we understand God's expectations when we interact with a needy one, when we see the face of a hungry or sick or crushed person? Whether or not we recognize Christ in the least powerful and most needy among us, we recognize our own neediness in the face of the one whose painful or oppressed condition tells us what is morally demanded. We know — perhaps too deeply for words — what we would want done if we were in that person's situation. This is more than obedience to a moral code: "Do to others as you would have them do to you" (Luke 6:31). This is not the same as John Rawls's philosophical theory that a community should decide its political and social rules according to an imagined least advantaged position.[18] The oppressed or hurting or hungry person who looks at us and conveys to us God's morality accuses us, and we *feel* it! There is pain or anger or hate or fear or disgust; there is *passion*. Passion can reach our inner depths where no knowledge of moral rules or philosophical and scientific reasoning can touch, where no societal prejudices or cultural norms can intrude. But even passion will not teach us God's morality or motivate us to moral response if we cannot identify with the neediness of the other. To do this, we must know our own neediness, our own dependence.

If our dependence — in the image of God's dependence — is accepted, then a reinterpretation of the Great Commandment is possible: "You shall love the Lord your God with all your heart, and with all your soul, and with all your strength, and with all your mind; and your neighbor as yourself" (Luke 10:27). In Luke's Gospel, after citing this law, the lawyer asks Jesus, "Who is my neighbor?" (10:29). The lawyer wants Jesus to tell him whom he should love and whom he can ignore. But in telling the story of the Good Samaritan, Jesus instead tells the lawyer that he must *be the neighbor* to whoever is in need. To love the neighbor as ourselves is empathetic response, based on the reality that self-concern is the essence of human survival. When we see not only Christ but ourselves in the one who is dependent on us for help, we respond because we know that our own dependent humanity requires such response. Thus our willingness to meet the needs of those who depend on us, the least powerful and most needy among us, is not obedience to external factors or divine command, but response to our own inner need to know that life can be caring, that we can trust one another.

Another of Jesus' teachings also takes on a different meaning when we hold up the mirrors of God's and humanity's dependence: "Love your enemies" (Luke 6:27a). Who is our enemy when we think about dependence? Our enemy is what we fear, what is embodied in the person who is dependent. We are threatened by the neediness of others — the person with severe disabilities, whose dependence reminds us that we too have been and will be dependent; the person dying with cancer or AIDS whose condition evokes in us the awareness that we too will die and in the process become utterly dependent on caretakers. We see a self-image that we want to deny in the enemy understood in this way. But if we accept our own dependence, we can turn this around. Such understandings of Christian teachings can provide the ethical insights needed not only for accepting and overcoming our own fear of dependence, but also for accepting and overcoming our fear and hate of those who depend on us. We can come to a point of tolerance rather than resentment about our own and others' dependence.

4

QUILTING

The Divine-Human Destiny of Cooperation

Quilting

I sat in the wooden rocking chair in the living room of the home where I was reared. A fire blazed warmly in the hearth. My stepmother deftly stitched quilt pieces in which the design was made by varying folds of the cloth. I never have been able to do needlework, and I admired her skill. Yet as she talked about how the group of retired women at the church was making the quilt to auction off at the annual bazaar, I began my own inner dialogue. "Why are all these retired but healthy and active women making work to keep themselves busy when there are so many human needs to be met?" Overwhelmed by the pain and despair of the poor, infirm, and dying people of my daily rounds as a public health nurse, still seeing vividly the broken-down housing of some of the places I had been earlier that day, I was angry at so much wasted human effort. "Why do these women not become politically active? Why are they not joining together in social action to make life better for the poor and oppressed?" As I tuned back into the conversation, I heard her say the money they raised would be sent to a national church fund for outreach ministry. My inner thoughts were only slightly more benevolent at the time. And even now I have problems with people who think in terms of only charity — usually administered by others — rather than a combination of charity and socioeconomic transformation of the structures that cause dehumanizing conditions. In retrospect, however, that quilt has become a precious gift to me.

Each woman worked at home to design and sew her sections of the quilt. The women came together on a weekday at the church to combine their efforts, map out their plans for the coming week, and enjoy the community that had come from their shared creativity toward a cause that enabled them to transcend their own time and place. I can see now that they were cooperating in their own small way in the work for God's promise in human history.

Sometimes I wonder if God's promised life might be much nearer if each of us were to join with others in communities to do just that much toward its fulfillment. I also wonder if these women understood that in their community of creativity they were voluntarily cooperating, pooling their time and talent, not only with one another but also with God. How sad that so few of us can think of ourselves as co-workers with God. Wouldn't that be gospel — good news — to so many whose work seems to them just wheel-spinning? Of course, such a realization might require that we ask whether our work *is* God's work.

Reflections such as this come out of my experiences of trying to piece together fragments of my faith with fragments of my public health work that often seemed too incongruous to be sewn into a single pattern. My graduate studies of conventional Christian ethics did nothing to mend the problem. The shared experiences and insightful writings of many women finally opened me to new understandings of the whole human enterprise. Womenviews have helped me to see the fragments of my faith and my public health nursing and my ethical studies as integrally related, all part of a quilt of life that is difficult to construct but possible and rewarding when God and humans are working with and empowering one another.

Images of Cooperation

The surroundings are humble, but the quilts that she displays by laying them across her lap are rich with color, design, and family tradition. An African-American woman sits in a wooden rocking chair in a small, tidy, unpainted frame house in the Southeast and proudly displays the quilts of generations of her foremothers. She shows how some designs have been repeated over the generations while others have been newly created; she compares the materials used in earlier quilts with those of more recent years. Each quilt is a family treasure, and each has a story. The quilt she has made is the most recent chapter in the story of her family, which had survived slavery. The images of this scene, first experienced several years ago when I was previewing a video[1] for use in an ethics class, continue to reach deeply within me.

The same video introduced me to two childless, aging, European-American sisters who have taken up quilting as their way to live on in the lives of their siblings' children and grandchildren. They began by making a wedding quilt for each niece and nephew. Then they made baby quilts for the next generation. Now they are making wedding quilts for that next generation, and as the numbers multiply they wonder if the new generation of babies will come faster than they can make the quilts. This quilting project has become their life's work. Large areas of their shared home are devoted to the materials from which they choose to make the designs that portray their lives in cloth and stitch for future generations. They work as a team on each quilt and are shown sitting together sewing different parts of a nearly finished work of art.

In contrast to these happy reasons for quilting is the NAMES Project AIDS Memorial Quilt, now made up of more than twenty thousand disconnected panels. Each panel is a memorial to a friend or family member who has died of AIDS. Numerous times since 1987, these testaments of grief have been spread out on the grassy expanses surrounding our national houses of government, museums, and monuments in Washington, D.C., rending the hearts of the thousands who watched, participated, or visited. Despite its tragic reason for being, the AIDS Memorial Quilt points to remarkable ventures in cooperation.

The NAMES Project was started in San Francisco in the spring of 1987 to remember persons who had died of AIDS, comfort grieving friends and relatives, and generate funds to support persons living with AIDS. People gathered at a storefront and sewed three-by-six-feet quilt panels as memorials to their loved ones lost to AIDS. Additional panels were sewn at home and donated. By late 1990 the quilt panels had been displayed in many locations, and more than a million and a half visitors had donated $800,000.[2] In October 1992, when the AIDS Memorial Quilt spread its signs of death and hope on the lawn in our nation's capital, it was "in conjunction with the largest gathering of AIDS-related service organizations and volunteers."[3]

Also in San Francisco was Trinity United Methodist Church, a small congregation that shared its facilities with a congregation of the United Metropolitan Community Church, whose majority membership is homosexual. The church building was destroyed by arson in 1981. The fire was believed to be due to the church's inclusion of people from several races and cultures, and its willingness to house a gay congregation. Since the two congregations did not have the resources to rebuild, they decided to try to find an organization with fund-raising capabilities that would share the costs and the space. A request was circulated for proposals from community organizations. The NAMES Project, housed in a nearby storefront, presented the winning proposal.[4]

The NAMES Project and Trinity Methodist Church formed a new corporation to be housed in a building on the property owned by the church. An international competition was held for an architectural design to meet the unique needs for storing and displaying the quilt panels and to provide appropriate space for various activities to take place in the building. Not only the two worshiping communities and the NAMES quilt but also several organizations to support and serve persons living with HIV/AIDS are part of what is called the Life Center Office.[5] Ironically, out of fire and death have come life, hope, and cooperation at its best.

Traditionally, quilting has been a group project. Women have gathered on a regular schedule for quilting bees, where they shared not only their time and talents but also their daily lives and hopes and dreams with one another. Today women continue to gather for such creative handicrafts, but a new kind of sisterhood has formed among women who gather to "hear one another into speech"[6] and do theology in concert. Can these be called "theological bees"? Other women's theologies are coming out of a different kind of cooperative effort, where each woman makes her contribution after the group has designed the project. This is more like the quilting story that I shared above and the AIDS Memorial Quilt.

Quilting conjures up many images: generational continuity; creative life out of destructive death; hope instead of despair; vision; newness from the old; dialogue; sisterhood; concerted effort. All provide important insights about being creative beings who need one another and cooperate to improve human life.

The writing of this chapter is itself a quilting project. Here many bits and pieces of theological and ethical fabrics are sewn together. Each is only a fragment but together they gradually become an overall design that reveals God to be a quilter of human life and ourselves to be God's co-quilters. This idea that we are God's co-quilters discloses a third aspect of being human — our participation in divine-human cooperation toward a moral destiny with God for justice and mercy.

Womenviews of Empowering Cooperation

The verb "to cooperate" is a combination of the Greek *koinos,* meaning common, and the Latin *operari,* meaning to work. Cooperation, then, means working with, being a co-worker on a common task.[7] The idea of working with God, of being God's co-workers in the quilting of human life, however, gives whole new meanings to the word. To embrace such a notion requires different understandings of ourselves in relation to one another and God.

Womenviews hold up exciting theological vistas for thinking about our being co-quilters of human life with God. Women, who create life and foster nurturing relationships of support, who bring together families and friends for meals, who gather to make quilts of warmth and beauty or to do theology in new ways, are especially aware of God's presence *in the midst of cooperative efforts toward liberation and justice.*

In this chapter I show that the spiritual empowerment of God comes when the cooperative work of a community takes it outside of itself to bring about justice and mercy for the larger society. My argument is informed by the work of Rita Nakashima Brock, who makes a convincing case that the Christic presence (God incarnate) is found in what she calls Christa/Community rather than just the person of Jesus or any individual person.[8] This Christic presence comes in the psychological healing ministry to one another in the community and applies to both the early Jesus community and the church of today. The primary difference in our two positions comes in the distinction between community and cooperation. She finds the Christic presence in what she calls the Christa/Community that ministers to its members and reaches out to heal and include others. I find God's presence in the interactions between people as they reach out to the outcasts who embody the needy and suffering Christ among us. In other words, I focus more on communities of outreach than communities of healing.

Cooperation, understood as co-quilting with God, changes the meaning and purpose of relationships and communities. The work that brings women together is what opens the way to community with both one another and God. Alida Verhoeven, a Dutch-Argentinean woman, expresses this powerfully:

> I'm not sure how to *think* of God, but I know that the help I've been given has helped me *feel* God; I feel a presence, a spiritual force around us, it moves us. I can't give it a form. It is a force that does not leave us alone. *It belongs to the space where we work together,* trying to ease the pain of these difficult times, listening to each other, supporting each other, and also constructively criticizing each other, always with the objective of building something better. That is what makes me feel like I'm worth something, and pushes me on.[9]

This "Spiritual Force," says Verhoeven, is a "vital-creative-presence for life" that is manifest when there is cooperative effort "that promotes life, love, justice, and peace."[10] Here the spiritual empowerment and sense of authority experienced in cooperative efforts are understood as arising from the interactions of the group itself. This empowerment is believed to be God.

This same sense that God is empowering presence in cooperative ventures is expressed in many ways by women from diverse situations. Beverly Wildung Harrison, in a conversation with other women engaged in a joint effort for liberating and just theological education, reveals her sense that justice "can't happen until the connections are being made, until others call you forth, connect with you, make you take yourself seriously or make you take them seriously." For Harrison, "it's a completely circular thing. God *is* in the connections."[11] Picturing a more inclusive and socially involved church, Sallie McFague adds that "in the model of the church we have sketched, God is present as our friend in all our companionable encounters with the world."[12]

The belief that God is present in and empowering our work with one another on behalf of others means that God is known among us in a different sense than that sketched in the previous chapter. God is the neighbor[13] who works with us to respond to the God who is in the least powerful and most needy among us. For Letty Russell, this realization "means that every person has become our partner." She points out that such partnership is our human destiny. We are created to participate with God in a new reality that requires commitment to cooperative partnerships whose tasks both transcend and connect the collective members.[14]

These womenviews of God's co-working and empowering presence invite a reconsideration of a part of the Christian tradition that has been problematic for women: the kingdom of God. Conventionally, the kingdom, a teaching that plays an important role in the Synoptic Gospels, has been understood as a promised time to come when God's law or God in Christ will rule in human history. Based on the hierarchical and all-powerful model of the roman emperor, New Testament kingdom sayings and teachings have led to portrayals of God in Christ as mighty ruler, Lord of heaven and earth, King of kings who one day will take control of human history and set it right either here on earth or in another kind of existence. Women, who are at the bottom of the hierarchy and also reject the masculine imagery of king to symbolize the God in whose image they too are created, have been searching for ways to recast these kingdom sayings, to speak of God's reign or commonwealth.

Attempts to resolve the problem come from many sources. Cuban-American feminist Ada María Isasi-Díaz uses the term "kin-dom" because "kingdom" presupposes God is male, and the concept of kingdom is both hierarchical and elitist. She also eschews the word "reign" for the latter reasons. "The word 'kin-dom' makes it clear that when the fullness of God becomes a day-to-day reality in the world at large, we will all be sisters and brothers — kin to each other."[15] Sharon Welch takes this same argument further. She rejects the kingdom language completely because it connotes "conquest, control, and final victory over the elements of nature as well as over the structures of injustice." Instead she thinks in terms of "the beloved community," which is the matrix within which "partial victories over injustice lay the groundwork for further acts of criticism and courageous defiance."[16] Commenting on the temptations of Jesus in Luke 4, Filipino biblical scholar Elizabeth Domínguez writes that Jesus rejects the offer of kingship: "Jesus has nothing to do with this kingly power, either — it is not power for life." She notes that immediately after rejecting the various uses of power to which he is tempted, Jesus proclaims the Jubilee Year.[17] She sees that not kingdom but a reordered society according to Jesus' tradition's scriptural visions and norms is the reason for Jesus' work and his call for co-workers.

Each of the above women's reinterpretations of kingdom language conveys the idea of a sociopolitical reality, a future time when God or God's law will rule in human history. In light of the views of God's creating and transcending, needing and waiting, empowering and co-working presence among us that have been pieced together from the womenviews explored and explicated in this book, a radically different interpretation of kingdom is required. Instead of the traditional reading — "the kingdom of

God is among you" (Luke 17:21) — the passage might be rendered more accurately to read: "The empowerment of God is among you." Certainly this is what the womenviews explored earlier in this chapter suggest — that God's empowerment is among us.

A thoroughgoing exegetical study might show that many of the kingdom sayings and parables lend themselves to such an alternative interpretation. In the limitations of this chapter, just one parable will be examined, and then some contemporary parables will be proposed. The parable to be considered is the one about leaven (Matt. 13:33; also Luke 13:20–21):

> The kingdom of heaven is like yeast that a woman took and mixed in with three measures of flour until all of it was leavened.

This parable was chosen because it has to do with women's work; but it is also helpful because it follows immediately after another parable that conveys a corresponding message: "The kingdom of heaven is like a mustard seed . . . " (Matt. 13:31–32); and it precedes the kingdom parables about treasure hidden in a field and fine pearls (Matt. 13:44–45), both of which might be interpreted to have similar meanings.

"What is being said about God's reign by the parable of the leaven?" asks biblical scholar Sharon Ringe. She notes that the parable tells about the task of making bread daily, and she ponders the details of that task: only a small amount of yeast is needed to bring to life a large amount of inert dough. The whole leavening process takes place in a way that is hidden. The yeast turns the dough into a living organism, so that it is no longer merely a product of human hands. The bread that will be baked meets the most basic of human needs. And the parable is drawn from the common household experiences of what was then solely women's work.[18] The usual idea of kingdom is challenged by this parable because nothing about the yeast or the woman's task of *daily* bread-making fits the idea of a mighty God's eternal reign. As Ringe sees, the details about yeast and women's work "are jarring when juxtaposed with the holiness of God's reign. In fact, they run counter to people's usual notions of what is appropriate to a 'reign,' and to normal human perceptions of power and majesty."[19]

Ringe's findings in this and other New Testament passages lead her to interpret "kingdom" in terms of Jubilee, the Jewish hope for a social order based on God's justice. Her understandings counter the idea of kingdom as the reign of God, but with Isasi-Díaz, Welch, and Domínguez she continues to think about kingdom as a sociopolitical reality. Womenviews allow a radically different reading. Instead of indicating a just society of human making, "kingdom" can mean empowerment for the work of justice. Thus a different rendering of the parable can be offered:

> The empowerment of God is like yeast that a woman took and mixed in with three measures of flour until all of it was leavened.

Since such empowerment is an ongoing presence with and for us, contemporary parables can convey the exciting and assuring message in alternative ways. I want to offer two such examples:

> The empowerment of God is like the needle that a woman uses to make her quilts. Without it she cannot sew but it is not visible in the finished work.

> The empowerment of God is like the bond between women who gather to sew quilts for their families and friends. Without their common bond the work would not happen, yet others can experience it only in the warmth and beauty of the covers they make.

If such an interpretation is accepted, then at least some of Jesus' teachings about the kingdom do not point to a sociopolitical reality — a future time or even an already but not yet time when God will rule in human hearts and history. Instead, the kingdom teachings are about the reality that God is and always will be giving us the power to be the humans we are created to be, just as God gave Jesus the power to exemplify being human for us. Thus the empowerment of God that Jesus taught about is not our moral destiny, not a goal to be sought or a time to be awaited. Rather, the empowerment of God is to be embraced like a precious gift, a buried treasure or fine pearls; it is the empowerment by which we are enabled to work with God and one another toward our common destiny.

This way of recasting kingdom language has major implications for being human and for Christian ethics. Kingdom ideas reinterpreted to mean empowerment raise questions about the goals, purposes, or ends of our common work with God, who is known in the midst of our cooperative work with neighbors. If our Christian work is not toward God's kingdom, what is our moral destiny?

Cooperation as Moral Destiny

Central to women's theological and ethical thinking is the deeply embraced belief that human beings are subjects or creative agents of our own destiny; we are not objects on which history acts. This already has been anticipated in the previous discussion, but here the focus is directed more specifically to the view that we humans are free to shape our individual and corporate destinies. Carter Heyward helps us *feel* it with a story:

> Once there was a wise old woman, a witch, who lived in a small village. The children of the village were puzzled by her — her wisdom, her gentleness, her strength, and her magic. One day several of the children decided to fool the old woman. They believed that no one could be as wise as everyone said she was, and they were determined to prove it. So the children found a baby bird and one of the little boys cupped it in his hands and said to his playmates, "We'll ask her whether the bird I have in my hands is dead or alive. If she

says it's dead, I'll open my hands and let it fly away. If she says it's alive, I'll crush it in my hands and she'll see that it's dead." And the children went to the old woman and presented her with this puzzle. "Old woman," the little boy asked, "this bird in my hands — is it dead or alive?" The old woman became very still, studied the boy's hands, and then looked carefully into his eyes. "It's in your hands," she said.[20]

Heyward follows this parabolic story with the declaration that "genuinely creative authority, sacred at its root, is in our hands. . . . It touches and often frightens us as it calls us forth to become more fully who we are already: interdependent and mutual participants in this journey we call life."[21] As subjects of our own destiny in this world, we find ourselves thrown back not only on our own resources but also on our co-workers — God in our neighbors.

Womenviews of human life have shown that God's empowering presence, God's sharing of power as co-working neighbor, is experienced in collective attempts toward liberation and justice, mercy and peace. To be truly human, to image the God in whose image we are made, means that we are to join together with God and one another in these kinds of efforts. Cooperation understood in this way is a compelling norm for Christian life.

Such a norm calls into question efforts by groups or institutions that are directed solely toward the members or the maintenance of the community. Too often communities and organizations focus their energies and resources on their own survival rather than on the enabling purposes for which they are formed. The church is no exception.

Two communities, whose very reason for existence is concern for others, exemplify the kind of cooperation that promotes liberation and justice and sends people forth into their worlds as fully human, empowered to meet the moral challenge of being God's creative co-workers. The consciousness raising that takes place in shelters for battered women enables women to embrace full humanity and refuse to continue a life that is less than human. These cooperative efforts are changing the institutions of marriage and family, law and economics. A similar form of consciousness raising that is found in Latin American base Christian communities serves the same purposes, resulting in radical sociopolitical transformation. The process helps oppressed people see that accepting the social conditions that crush them is accepting an existence that is less than human, less than God created them to be. Both the battered women's shelters and the base Christian communities motivate people to become subjects of their own destinies, rather than objects of their abusers, oppressors, or exploiters.

These kinds of cooperative efforts offer models of what all human communities should be. They provide norms against which to measure societal institutions such as family, church, schools, business, or government and decide whether they are structured with the intent of enabling people to become fully human, co-creators of our common destiny. These models suggest that if our institutions do less, or if they promote ideologies, beliefs, or practices that serve to keep people in less than human status, then they are barriers to full humanity.

The women whose views have been considered above embrace our role as subjects of human history; they do not wait for God to intervene and transform the world. They see that in order to undertake the work of being subjects of our destinies, we need communities that cooperate for purposes beyond their own existence. Yet the questions remain: What are these purposes? What is our moral destiny? Is there some goal toward which we are working, or is life a collection of disconnected and unrelated quilt squares?

Anticipations of moral vision already have been seen. Working together for liberation and justice has been the context in which God's empowering and cooperating presence has been experienced. The vision of Jubilee, found in Hebrew and Christian scriptures, also has been mentioned.

In the writings examined for this book, the most passionate visions of future hope come from the women whose lived realities are farthest from their fulfillment. Chung Hyun Kyung writes that "Asian women know they cannot endure meaningless suffering if they do not dream of a world defined by wholeness, justice, and peace. They also know they will perish without a vision of life in its fullness and in its deepest beauty."[22] She then says that Asian women yearn "for the 'community of the harmonious life on earth,' where people 'regain the image of God,' and where 'all kinds of animals and [hu]mankind together live in harmony' and 'they shall not hurt or destroy' (Isa. 11:6–9)."[23]

Virginia Fabella, from the Philippines, and Sun Ai Lee Park, originally from North Korea, claim that we can change the face of the earth only if we work together. They envision women and men in cooperative communities of mutuality and reciprocity, with the common task of caring "not only for people but for our whole planet earth." They imagine "a new world; a transformed world; a world that truly mirrors God's design; a just, caring, and peace-filled world — indeed, a new creation."[24]

Vision must be tempered by reality, say first-world women. Sharon Welch cautions that if we assume we can ensure the results of our actions we will find ourselves paralyzed when faced with complex social problems. She notes that when confronted with problems they cannot solve, many people choose to make no moral response at all. They cannot even think of taking actions that render only partial solutions. She advocates an "ethic of risk" that encourages the undertaking of whatever limited actions or partial solutions are possible.[25]

Rosemary Radford Ruether finds in the Jubilee Year, as set forth in Leviticus 25 and Isaiah 61, and proclaimed by Jesus at the inauguration of his ministry in Luke 4, a source for moral vision that guards against thinking that we can accomplish once and for all our hopes and dreams for human life. She recognizes that "women who have been in charge of the repetitive tasks of daily clean-up and nurture are perhaps more able to see this than men."[26] Ruether points out that the Jubilee, which is supposed to be a reordering of society every fifty years, assumes change, backsliding, and the need to restructure periodically to reestablish justice and equality. As Ruether emphasizes, the Jubilee is not a return to some idealized past; rather, it is the reform needed for a just and livable society. New cultures and technologies, new situations and human needs will require a different vision for each new age. We are not called into partnership with God "to create the revolution once and for all, but to create the revolution for this generation."[27]

Third-world women offer visions of a re-created world. First-world women caution that our finitude stands in the way of achieving such hoped-for futures. As Christians, we need both passionate and utopian visions of liberation and justice heard from women who are most oppressed and also cautionary guidance from women who already are living in more just and liberating situations.

To be human, then, is to image God who is neighbor in the midst of us whenever we gather and elicit our transcending creativity for the common tasks of being the neighbor. To be faithfully human is not to accomplish our goals but always to work toward the goals God sets before us as the transcending and creating, needing and waiting, empowering and cooperating One *among us.* If enough of us faithfully live this way, there will be changes in our world; injustice will be mitigated, and the oppressed will be more liberated.

Yet the tragic dimensions of life cannot be overcome. Being fully human means that we do not let ourselves succumb to the despair of seeing only the failures but always look for God in the creative and cooperative work that human life depends on for its continued existence. The AIDS Memorial Quilt is a model of a creative, interdependent, cooperative response to human tragedy. This kind of response to the tragic and limiting realities of life is our destiny. We must live into the visionary promise of a just and merciful world at the same time that we recognize our inability to overcome all injustice and pain in human life.

Like the women whose quilts are passed down from generation to generation, our task is to accomplish what we can in our time and place. Yet we know that our quilts wear out and rot over time. We can learn from this experience of earthly existence that our purpose is not to achieve some goal of human history once and for all, but constantly to work together toward a vision of what human life is intended to be. This is our moral destiny.

5

WEAVING

Power at the Intersections

Weaving

Reflections on my own experiences provided artistic images for ethics in the three preceding chapters. Weaving, the image evoked for the art of ethics in this chapter, is autobiographical in a different way. My Scottish heritage and my love of the woolen tartans designed and woven by my ancestors offer an additional metaphor for the artistic work of ethics. I can imagine the care that went into preparing and dying the wool just the right color for the clan's signature plaids, the precision involved in keeping the proper tension in the looming process so that the cloth would be uniform in texture, and the memory and skill required to introduce new colors of yarn at just the right places. I can sense the warmth and protection of the beautiful woolen cloth.

Weaving is a practical art that produces clothing from many fibers. Historically, women spun fibers into thread or yarn and wove them into cloth, with which they fashioned their families' clothing. Today, mechanized processes in large factories have replaced women sitting at spinning wheels and hand looms in their homes. Some hand weaving of colorful tartans from wool continues in Scotland, however, and since that is part of my heritage, I find in it imagery for further explorations into womenviews of human life.

The weaving of tartans involves several steps. First, the wool is cut, cleaned, dyed the many colors of a family's distinguishing plaid, and spun into yarns. Then the loom is prepared carefully as the different colors of warp yarn are strung on it, so that the several colors of woof (or weft) yarn can be woven in their turn between alternating threads of the warp. As the yarns are woven into plaids, the assorted colors of yarn intersect, and blocks of new colors are created in the cloth along with blocks of the yarn colors. The dominant colors of one of my family's tartans are flame red, hunter green, and sky blue. Blocks of these colors are clearly visible in the finished cloth, but where red and green intersect, muddy blacks appear;

where green and blue meet, aqua shades are added; and where red and blue cross one another, soft violets are made.

Power at the Intersections

In this chapter, the strands of human life that were prepared in the three earlier chapters are woven together. When these distinct strands are interwoven, additional moral insights are discovered at the intersections. The weaving together of transcending creativity, dependence, and cooperation reveals power to be a central facet of human life and a crucial concern for Christian ethics.

Power as a characteristic of human life was implicit in the three previous chapters. To be created in God's image as one who creates life and transcends barriers to life is to be given the inner power of survival by God. Powerlessness was tacit in the chapter on dependence, which held up God's needing and waiting for our response as well as our need to accept ourselves as dependent beings in God's image. Power found in concert with others was explicit in the chapter on cooperation, where God's enabling presence with us was recognized. Such power and powerlessness, as constitutive of human life, are morally neutral.

Our appropriation and uses of power, however, are not morally neutral; they have profound theological and ethical importance. A first moral question has to do with our appropriation of power. The reinterpretation of the kingdom parable in the foregoing chapter lifts up the empowerment of God as a gift to be embraced and employed for God's work of liberation and justice in the world. At the same time, the womenviews that have been explored throughout this book suggest that we must not seek God's power for ourselves; we can only seek to be faithful to our humanity and our moral destiny and trust that God's power will be found in and among us. Thus power is imparted to us as a means to an end beyond itself, but power is not seen as an end to be sought.

Far more complex moral questions arise in relation to our utilization of power. The powers that are ours as creatures made in God's image give us capability and potential. Our powers constitute agency that has profound moral implications when exercised and thus warrant careful consideration.

Much of human history has been shaped by beliefs that human power is wielded as mastery over individuals and groups and over our natural environment. These beliefs about power as mastery have been reinforced both theologically and structurally. The results have been dehumanizing for all of us and increasingly threaten our very existence. For this reason, many women have questioned power exercised as domination and control and have attempted to offer alternative views.

Traditional Christian doctrines and teachings arose at a time when Western societies were structured in hierarchical ways that supported and glorified the powers of imperial sovereigns and manor lords. In such a culture, the concepts that were used to image the experience of God's power in history reflected the most powerful persons in the social order. These culturally determined ideas have led to beliefs that God is the dominant One and we are to be submissive before this all-powerful Other, in a master/servant kind of relationship. These beliefs in God's absolute power over us have continued to be upheld by some contemporary Christians. Such understandings of God often have contributed to dehumanizing perceptions and uses of power.

As Sharon Welch recognizes, even though portrayals of God as having absolute power over the creation are "intended to relativize all human claims to power, the valorization of domination and submission leads to the legitimization of imperial power."[1] When God is portrayed as the all-powerful Other who rules over us, a hierarchical ordering of human life is legitimized, albeit inadvertently. Such an ordering places people who have attained power by whatever means in positions to dominate and exploit others who are seen as, or rendered, less powerful. Our belief that we are created in God's image has encouraged us to act as we believe God acts. If we hold that God acts by controlling or dominating human beings, we will find in that belief justification for our doing the same.

Many women are offering creative alternatives to the perception of power/powerlessness as dominance/submission. The womenviews already considered in this book show that God is experienced and imaged not as a transcendent and wholly other power over us, but as a co-creating and co-transcending power within us. God is perceived and defined in the womenviews of this book not as an independent and self-sufficient power above human history, but as the needing and powerless One among us who depends on us. God is known and described in womenviews not as a power that descends into human life, but as a co-working neighbor who shares and evokes power in efforts of liberating justice. By recognizing God's power in these interactive ways, womenviews call into question beliefs about God's coercive, dominating, and controlling power over us. The power of mastery is neither a viable view of God nor a healthy norm for humans who image God. Thus women are reimaging both divine and human power in ways that clearly evidence our belief that if we are created in God's image and if God is incarnate in human history, then we cannot dichotomize power into God's and ours.

Such reimaging of power is central to third-world women's writings. Disempowered by their cultures, their families, and even their churches, they nevertheless find empowerment in God. Chung Hyun Kyung writes: "The power of God evokes in Asian women a distinct kind of power, which has been lost in patriarchal religion and society."[2] Chung poetically elaborates on the kind of power she finds in God:

> The power that fosters life rather than death,
> the power of working together,
> the power of experiencing one's true feelings,
> the power of acclaiming others and
> enabling them to realize their full
> potential as human beings.[3]

The power Chung celebrates is not power over us from above but power within us endowed by God who is among us; it is shared power or empowerment.

Third-world women often express God's power in terms of the Holy Spirit, which is associated with the "power of God *in community*."[4] Crescy John of India writes that women who are agents of change in the Asian setting rely on the Holy Spirit as a source of help and guidance. Drawing from numerous New Testament passages that promise this empowering presence for us, she shows, first, that God as Spirit is a trailblazer who leads us to truth and the future; second, that the Spirit strengthens and counsels us and serves as an advocate; and, third, that God in Spirit inspires and motivates us, and gives us spiritual gifts. She then declares that we are to be pliable instruments through which the Spirit can work to bring about changes in human history.[5]

A woman of Brazil reinterprets the Spirit in feminine and maternal terms. María Clara Bingemer believes that the Spirit understood in maternal ways opens us to be receptacles of God's grace in the same way we were nurtured by our mothers. A maternal view of the Spirit also "makes it possible for us to feel that we 'are not only *under* God but *in* God.'" Bingemer goes on to show that the empowering Spirit in *whom* we find ourselves is bestowed for our cooperation in God's work of justice and mercy in the world.[6]

First-world women also are reinterpreting power. In *Our Passion for Justice*, Carter Heyward writes: "God's power is ours — to the extent that we choose to make this tender power in-carnate in history."[7] In a later work, Heyward notes that Christianity rarely has emphasized God's *"deeply creative power, at once human and divine, as historically and ontologically embodied among us, transacted between and among ourselves daily as cocreative agents upon whom the power of love in history depends."*[8]

German theologian Bärbel von Wartenberg-Potter points out that Jesus modeled a different way to exercise God's gift of power. She sees that in Jesus, God's power was manifest not as all-powerful ruler, but as power of another order. This other order of power was based on compassion and love. "The sharp and prophetic critique which Jesus exercised arose out of a compassionate heart and a clearly focused love. This is the only thing Jesus possessed by way of power — it is the only power we, too, will have, if we follow him."[9]

Two recent American feminist works are devoted explicitly to the question of power; each modifies conventional understandings of power in a different way. Anna Case-Winter compares traditional male views of divine power with Charles Hartshorne's process theology and feminist theology, and then constructs what she calls a "process-feminist synthesis."[10] Case-Winter rejects the view that God's power is coercive, a matter of dominance and control, and thinks instead of relational and influencing or persuasive power. She argues that this power operates in the same way that the mind is persuaded by what it knows. Her primary concern is to reimage God's omnipotence (all-powerfulness) in ways that escape the problems of dominant, controlling power without reducing God's powerfulness. By thinking of power as persuasion, she can reinterpret omnipotence to mean "the capacity to influence *all* and to be influenced by *all*."[11]

In her "Christology of erotic power," Rita Nakashima Brock, however, criticizes even such persuading uses of power. While power understood as influence does move away from coercion and control, and does suggest mutuality and egalitarianism, says Brock, "it continues to connote the actor who may intentionally affect another's behavior through an effective use of the power she or he possesses."[12] Brock believes that as an alternative to such unilateral uses of power, "we must move from seeing power as a commodity possessed by a self toward seeing it as the bonds which create and sustain, and are recreated and sustained by relational selves."[13]

In contrast to both Case-Winter and Brock, womenviews as seen in this book unequivocally affirm the agency that is inherent in power and powerlessness within ourselves and in the empowerment of cooperative work with God and our neighbors. Such power, however, need not be seen as a commodity or possession that is used unilaterally to affect others in persuasive or coercive ways. The moral question, then, centers on how our God-given gifts of power and powerlessness can be exercised in ways that are faithful.

Women's experiences of creativity in giving birth, their recognition of the powerlessness inherent in dependence on one another, and their awareness of God's empowering presence with us for the life-giving work of justice and mercy lead to an interactive way of using power that is like midwifery. The midwife has no power to bring to birth new life from a woman in labor. She acts not *on* the mother, but *with* her. The mother alone has the capacity to bring about the birth, but the midwife's agency is required so that the mother can concentrate on her very physical part of the birthing process and not have to be concerned about logistical matters. Because the midwife's use of power is in her assistance to a mother who herself brings forth the new life, power modeled on midwifery functions only insofar as it operates with another to enable completion of a common goal, fulfillment of a joint purpose. A midwifery way of interacting is bilateral or multilateral, rather than unilateral; midwifery evokes power from another in concert with her. With midwifery there is not a more powerful subject acting upon a less powerful object; both are subjects of the empowering event. Midwifery cannot control; its effectiveness is in letting go, in becoming powerless, so as to allow another to become more powerful and take control of her own life. When our power is exercised as midwifery we are not diminished nor do we diminish the other. Instead, the power of both parties grows proportionately to the degree that a goal is accomplished in unison.

The interactional model of power exemplified as midwifery stands in sharp contrast to the unilateral mastery over others that has been the prevalent way to attain and use power in Western culture. Power exercised according to a mastery model is power wielded over others or over nature in a dominating or controlling way. Power appropriated and exploited as mastery usually is perceived as zero-sum power; if one person gains power, another person loses power proportionately. Thus the dominating person cannot empower those who are being dominated. Instead, to protect power, the person acting in the master's domineering ways diminishes the power of whatever or whoever is being controlled. Therefore, this way of using power oppresses and belittles, harms and destroys.

The persuasive or influencing use of power proposed by Case-Winter can be aligned with either mastery or midwifery. If the former, it coerces by intellectual or social means rather than by the use of force. If the latter, it can be a natural extension of the birthing process, the nurturing care that evokes growth and learning. Persuasion as a way of wielding power, however, is a manifestation of a midwifery model only if all parties have equal power. Teachers in both academia and the church who eschew the master/student model of instruction and attempt to employ methods that empower the students to be co-teachers and co-learners are coming close to midwifery ways of using power. But as long as the relationship is one in which the teacher has authority by virtue of her institutional role, a true manifestation of a midwifery approach to persuasion is precluded. Furthermore, mastery power can be exercised both forcefully and gently in the guise of a midwifery model.

Power utilized in midwifery's interactional ways leads to reinterpretations of God's use of power, which often is portrayed in terms of absolute mastery. If mastery power cannot empower others without being diminished, however, the possibility that God can be understood as almighty ruler, lord and master of all, is called into question. Such conceptions of God's power in relation to human history are incongruent with our experience of God's gift of power in and among us; they also counter Christian beliefs that God's power is everlasting and never-failing. The belief that Christ in the least among us is powerless — waiting, needing, and depending on our response — also is contrary to the idea that

God acts in controlling and diminishing ways. If God's power is enacted through midwifery means, however, such contradictions do not arise. With the interactive model of the midwife, God's power is increased rather than decreased precisely because God's co-working presence and Christ's powerlessness among us evoke power at the human–divine–human intersections of our lives. God as midwife has not only everlasting but also ever-growing power. We who are created in God's image are inheritors of the gift and the obligation of midwifery ways of applying our powers.

Despite such revised understandings of power, the realities of our world require the use of power in the form of persuasion or even control in certain circumstances. In childbirth, the midwife might have to persuade a woman to cooperate, or she might have to take control of a situation to protect mother and baby. No parent can abstain from taking control when her small child is endangered; and a parent also uses persuasion both tenderly and demandingly.

These too can be ways of imaging God's power under some circumstances. Exodus says that at the birthing of the Israelite nation, God had to persuade Moses to accept the calling to deliver his people before God became the co-working and co-empowering Holy One with the Israelites. And the Hebrews believed that God's mastery power was responsible for the plagues that finally accomplished their release from enslavement. Later, the prophets portrayed God as an anguished parent trying to discipline and persuade wayward children. Such uses of power by God, however, occur in the context of God's midwifery work to bring life out of danger in concert with the chosen people. Control and persuasion are employed toward the end of midwifery.

Once midwifery is recognized as a way of interacting that most nearly reflects the experience of God's power, the ways we accept and employ our powers in situations where we have authority and influence must be transformed. Instead of following the usual patterns of mastery, which include disempowering others or coercion of others to change their behavior, authority and influence can be transformed if they are utilized in ways that empower others as does a midwife. Thus we can exercise our authority and influence to be *co*-creators, *co*-dependents, and *co*-workers if our means are guided and judged by midwifery ways of using power and our ends are the interactive empowerment of both others and ourselves.

Nevertheless, power in any configuration of control or persuasion is at best morally ambiguous. Our lives are permeated with the damages from wrongful uses of power. When misused, power can cause death, torture, oppression, and war. Abused children and battered wives; oppression in the name of order; war justified as a means to peace; democracy and free-market capitalism foisted on nations that are not yet prepared — all these are symptoms of power gone awry. These realities lead to a troubling question: Can we exercise our inherent powers in ways that are not contrary to what it means to be human, to be creatures made in God's image?

Womenviews of dependence provide a necessary balance to our freedom in the use of power. God's dependence on us for divine-human work in this world tempers God's power over us; our dependence on one another can temper our use of power in relation to one another. If we can accept our need for others, and more fundamentally our dependence on a community of persons on whom we can rely for our needs to be met, then the way we use our power in relation to others is held in some kind of equilibrium. The tension present in our recognition of dependence can be a deterrent to prevent us from destroying others or reducing others to a status that renders them unable to be mutual partners in the work of our world. Such respect for others, born of our need for one another, also can deter us from pushing our ideas, beliefs, values, and norms onto others — a kind of persuasion or influence that might better be called intellectual coercion.

When power is wielded in ways that are not both guided by the interactive model of midwifery and also tempered by acceptance of our common neediness, it causes chronic and seemingly unsolvable problems in human communities of every size. The abusive father may one day need the tender and loving care of his child; but unless the child has been nurtured and loved, that care cannot be expected. The denigrating husband, who destroys his wife's self-image, may find that she no longer is capable of meeting his needs. These familial patterns are applicable to the larger society if we recognize our dependence on others.

Just one example may suffice to illustrate the idea. For centuries nations in the Northern Hemisphere have exploited and denigrated peoples in the Southern Hemisphere in order to gain the riches and enhanced life-style of Western culture. This has been done through the use of both controlling and persuading power. Now we are realizing that these oppressed nations are a burden on the whole Northern Hemisphere. Our exploitation of power has led us to a situation where we are in danger of losing what we have gained because there are shrinking markets for our goods and ever-increasing demands on our financial resources to rectify the damages. Just as threatening is the loss of trust that our behavior has provoked. Power exercised in dominating and persuading ways can have devastating effects when it weakens or destroys the foundations for a world community where we can trust that others will meet our needs.

The power that is revealed at the intersections of transcending creativity, dependence, and cooperation is a characteristic of human life that has central moral importance. This power arises from the norms explored in earlier chapters, yet has its own moral standing alongside the previous norms. Thus the unconventional mirrors of part 1 reflect four distinct ethical guidelines for Christian life: transcending creativity, dependence, cooperation, and power. These will have specific relevance for part 2.

A Particular Pattern for Ethics

The image of the Scottish tartan provides an important qualifier for the work of this book. As early as the 1500s, particular colors of plaids were common to discrete areas of the Scottish Highlands because the wools were dyed from whatever plants were available locally. By the nineteenth century, unique colors and patterns came to be associated with certain families from specific districts of both the Highlands and the Lowlands of Scotland.[14] The tartan, then, provides an imagery of something that is created for a particular place and people.

The work of this book is for a particular place and people. As I said at the beginning, my life experiences called forth this book. The theological ethics that have been worked out in womenviews of human life were motivated particularly by my remembered pain and existential reality during eleven years of public health nursing. The normative views of Christian life found in part 1 of this book have been formulated with these particular problems in mind.

Theology and ethics always must be designed to address particular problems. A single moral pattern that will suffice as a frame of reference for looking at any and all human situations cannot be derived from the past or the present; from womenviews, menviews, or both; from first-world, third-world, or global perspectives. Even though the theological insights and moral norms of part 1 might provide ethical guidelines for other issues and crises, I did not have other purposes in mind when I was writing. I am offering one possible moral pattern with which to think ethically and respond morally to the particular social crises addressed in part 2.

The moral perspectives provided in this book also are particular in that I am part of the privileged-oppressor, white middle class and yet my choice of an ethical standing point is with the poor, oppressed, and marginalized persons — many of them people of color — whom I served as a public health nurse. My social location contradicts my ethical location, thus placing me somewhere between the two. From this midpoint I try to speak authentically as a Christian woman to those who have ears to hear.

Despite my chosen location for doing ethics, my views probably would not be found fitting by people who suffer from the social crises to be considered. Even though all of the problems addressed in part 2 are my passionate concerns, I have not been oppressed by any of them. I hope that in some sense I am in solidarity with those who are hurt by these social crises. I want to speak *on their behalf;* but I cannot speak *for* them. Only those who actually suffer the pains pondered in part 2 can speak authentically for themselves.

With these stipulations, then, moral reflection on mothers on welfare; women facing reproductive choices; and persons with addictions, handicapping conditions, or catastrophic diseases can begin. Yet this is not a departure from Christian ethics in order to do the practical work of the world. As the social crises under consideration in part 2 are engaged, the womenviews of human life explored in part 1 take on new meanings. At the same time, the womenviews of human life worked out in part 1 allow ethical reflection on the social crises addressed in part 2, which pointedly highlights some of the moral crises of our culture.

PART TWO

Impassioned and Reasoned Responses to Social Crises

In the stories that begin each chapter of part 2, names and other iden-tifying information have been changed to protect the privacy of the persons. Because these accounts were not recorded at the time, they are told from memory; this has meant that some details were lost to me, and I have had to fill out the stories with composite pictures from my larger experiences with similar situations in public health nursing.

6

WELFARE
Recognizing Reproductivity

Feeling the Pain

I was on my first home visit as a public health nurse. When I approached the slender, two-story brick house I noted how narrow it was, situated starkly on a lot with no shrubbery or trees. Inside, I realized that the house was just as shallow as it was narrow. We sat in a living-dining-kitchen room that was crowded with minimal furniture and felt packed with two adults and three small children occupying it. In conversation I learned that the second floor consisted of two tiny bedrooms and a bath.

The physical limitations of the house were difficult to absorb, but the emotional impact was almost overwhelming: a mother and her twelve children lived in this cramped space. After several marriages and other relationships, Elizabeth was trying to survive on Aid to Families with Dependent Children (AFDC) in this house with her children who ranged in age from two to seventeen. Already emotionally shaken by these realities, I looked down at the records I held on my lap and realized for the first time that Elizabeth and I were born on the same day. Inwardly I was reeling. At thirty-five, I had three children ranging in age from eight to thirteen. We did not live in luxury, but the comparison was painful to make. I tried to imagine what it would be like to cope with the life Elizabeth endured daily, and I was repelled by the very thought.

As the March afternoon sunlight dimmed, roaches began coming out from their hiding places. I moved my bag and shooed them away from my feet. In the midst of these physical and emotional stresses, I tried to carry on a conversation with this struggling mother of twelve about one of her sons who was physically handicapped and needed surgical correction. She obviously was unable to deal with the need to take her son to the clinic at a children's hospital in a nearby city. She had no car, and public transportation was limited, requiring many transfers and waits. She did not have the money for the trip. She had no one to watch the other children while she and this child went away for a day, much less for longer times when the surgical procedures would be done. She thought she might be able to manage it in the summer, when her teenage children could watch the younger children. I pointed out to her that if she broke the appointment scheduled for mid-April, it would be the fourth cancellation, and her son would be dropped from the state-funded program. She shrugged and said, "Well, I guess he'll just have to go through life crippled."

My initial response was to think of Elizabeth as negligent. While driving my car to another visit, however, I began to absorb the realities of her plight, and I understood that she was in a situation that forced her to make choices I would not make. I was determined to convince the clinic to reschedule her son shortly after school was out, so she would have at least one barrier removed. The reality was, however, that every mother wanted her child to be seen in the summer, either because she did not want the child to miss school or because she had more family or neighborhood baby-sitters available during school vacations.

Elizabeth's location made her life especially difficult. She lived in a single-family home in an isolated area without neighbors who had common problems. In contrast, most of the other mothers on AFDC whom I served lived in subsidized apartments, surrounded by other families with similar problems. This afforded them a community that came to the rescue by baby-sitting, borrowing a car to drive a neighbor and her children to the clinic, or otherwise offering a helping hand.

The number of children also contributed to Elizabeth's difficulties. In my eleven years of public health nursing, I found that most mothers on welfare had from one to three children; only occasionally did I encounter mothers with as many as six or more children. Younger women who had access to better birth control and (after 1973) abortion, and who aspired to a life beyond the home, tried to limit their families.

Many of Elizabeth's difficulties were not unique even though she was isolated and overburdened with children. Inadequate housing; single parenting; part-time, low-paying jobs to supplement insufficient welfare payments; and dealing with belittling government agencies — all these made women trying to raise their children on AFDC feel like aliens. Their estrangement from the society in which they lived and sometimes were employed grew more marked in the years of my public health nursing, from 1970 to 1981, as the vision for the War on Poverty faded and funds dried up. As resources became scarce at the end of the 1970s and into the 1980s, I saw the pain of all mothers on welfare grow more acute. The past decade has exacerbated the problems as the buying power of AFDC and related benefits has steadily declined.

Seeing the Realities

We live in a world that blames women if anything goes wrong in their lives, be it rape or divorce or children with problems. Consequently women are culturally conditioned to blame themselves.[1] Women who find themselves in need of AFDC are subject to heavy doses of such blame from without and within. Yet even a superficial examination of the realities uncovers some of the multiple forces that are at play in the impoverishment of women and children in America, many of whom try to survive on AFDC for at least brief and transitional periods.

Pamela Sparr reports that in 1982, "women constituted an estimated 61 percent of adults (people fifteen years and older) who were living in poverty. Nearly one half of all poor families were headed by single women."[2] In 1988, Mimi Abramovitz observed that women and their children were "the prime recipients of AFDC, not only because so many [were] poor, but also because [in almost half the states] only children with an absent parent [were] eligible for the program."[3] Even in states that do allow AFDC with a father in the home, the father must be unemployed for the family to qualify. If he earns any income at all, even though it could not possibly support the family, then AFDC and other benefits are denied.[4] Therefore, most AFDC recipients are single mothers with dependent children.

Numerous reasons undergird the need for so many women to turn to welfare programs for survival. Here two of them will be surveyed summarily: first, some factors contributing to women's economic needs and then, several culturally spawned attitudes that sustain women's shaky economic situations. Thereafter, a brief examination of a few interlocking systemic factors that complicate welfare programs for women and children will show that America needs a different approach.

Socioeconomic Factors

Economic inequalities lead women to seek financial support from government agencies. Traditionally women have worked in low-paying jobs at wages that might supplement a husband's income but could not provide for a family. Despite some advances, most women's employment continues to yield wages that cannot support a family.[5] Even highly educated women who teach in grade school or work in other serving and nurturing professions seldom earn a family wage. When single women with minimal education or job skills have to seek employment to maintain themselves and their children, even if they find jobs they often live at or below the welfare level, which in most states is itself well below the official poverty level.[6] They find that their meager salaries or minimum-wage paychecks are soon consumed by health care needs, food costs, transportation to and from work, and child care; and they face a disintegrating family due to their absence and fatigue from trying to raise children without adequate resources or assistance.[7] In my own experiences with mothers receiving Aid to Families with Dependent Children, the most frequently cited reasons for choosing welfare rather than employment as a means of livelihood were the costs of child care and health insurance.

Many factors lead to women's needs for economic resources in the first place. The growing necessity for women to supplement the incomes of their husbands or live-in partners will not be included here, although this is a major reason women have entered the labor market in such large numbers.[8] The focus will be on the single mother who finds she is unable to sustain herself and children due to deficient education, lack of job training, or low wages.

Some women find themselves impoverished due to abandonment or divorce by the fathers of their children. On average, when men no longer provide for families, their incomes rise 30 percent while their wives and children find themselves trying to exist on 70 percent less money.[9] Little if any attention has been paid to the loss of the breadwinner ethic that contributes so heavily to abandonments and divorces. Men's repudiation of the breadwinner ethic is cited by Barbara Ehrenreich as a major factor contributing to increasing numbers of women and children needing AFDC for subsistence. According to Ehrenreich, male flight from breadwinning responsibilities began in the 1950s, fueled by a set of values promoted by *Playboy* and related media sources. "By the end of the 1970s," she reports, "the old ideological props for the male breadwinner ethic had crumbled. Today the man who postpones marriage and avoids women who are likely to become financial dependents is considered not deviant but healthy."[10] Over the past decade, loss of the breadwinner ethic has been joined by loss of breadwinner wages due to changes in the economy. This is especially true of working-class men of color. As a result, more and more men — married or otherwise — are forsaking their duties to women and children. In this misogynous culture, we are quick to blame women, or the women's liberation movement, for the growing number of women who are single heads of families. Instead, we need to place an appropriate amount of blame on the failure of many men to accept family responsibilities and the failure of our economy to support families. Women left with insufficient financial resources due to abandonment or divorce by their husbands or partners usually have not chosen to be independent of male support.

Some women, however, do choose to be single heads of families. Given the economic parsimony of both women's wages and AFDC payments, women who make this choice usually are deciding that it is the lesser of two evils. In my public health nursing I encountered two very different groups of women for whom this was the case.

First, I found that some young women got pregnant, left their parental families, and applied for welfare because the family situation was so traumatic. Sometimes the woman's father or her mother's male friend had abused her. Sometimes her mother, a single head of household, had been stressed beyond her coping abilities by poverty and family, and had become abusive. Sometimes the house was so crowded that privacy or simply personal space was sought. Some young women, even teenagers, chose to get pregnant because it was the only creative, productive option they saw for themselves as they were failing in schools that did not meet their needs or were looking at shrinking employment opportunities.[11] To middle-class readers, such choices may seem mistaken at best and exploitative of the welfare system at worst. Yet statistics reported in 1988 showed that, on average, welfare benefits were continued just over two years, after which mothers made a fresh start through job training, education, or marriage, and were no longer economically dependent on the state.[12] More recent statistics show the average length of AFDC coverage is 6.6 years.[13] Perhaps this increase reflects the loss of employment opportunities for men and women, and cutbacks in job training and other programs designed to benefit the impoverished populations that more often have to turn to AFDC for support.

Other women, the second group, chose to be single heads of families for reasons that were quite different but just as tragic. Women who were abused by male partners, or who saw their children being abused by them, often chose to live without a man as the source of economic sustenance. Battered women's networks assisted such women in finding housing and financial backing. Often, due to their lack of job experience, the low wages women usually earn, and/or the very young ages of their children, the women escaped a battering man only to face the hardships of AFDC and its social stigma.

When women choose welfare sustenance for whatever reason, they become disenfranchised workers, observes Theresa Funiciello:

> They perform what is supposed to be a socially valued service, but they receive neither adequate compensation nor respect. Instead of having their labor viewed as "mothering" they are labeled as dependent. The result is often defeating. The women become increasingly more insecure, and their lowered self esteem makes the transition out of welfare an even greater hurdle.[14]

Clearly, women and children who are impoverished and have to exist on welfare are not in a very healthy situation.

Cultural Factors

Why are AFDC funds so meager, well below the poverty level in almost every state? Why is there such a social stigma attached to welfare support for mothers? Facing the cultural attitudes surrounding the social stigma will reveal some of the reasons why AFDC benefits are so low.

In our culture, the kind of work women do in the home has little or no social or economic value. If a woman works in someone else's home to provide child care, cooking, and cleaning services, she will be paid a low salary. The same jobs done in a woman's own home are not even considered work. Women accrue no income while they are working as homemakers and therefore are entitled to no Social Security or retirement except through their husbands' benefits. Yet divorce or abandonment can leave a woman who worked in the home all her life with little or no economic security in old age.[15]

We speak of "working mothers" — meaning those who go outside the home and earn a salary — as if mothers do no work in the home. Yet women provide the most basic needs of human existence in their child care and nurturing roles. I used to tell expectant mothers in prenatal classes that the work they were doing in pregnancy, and would continue to do in a different way after giving birth, was far more important than the ships, bridges, or roads the fathers of their children were building or the stores, banks, or factories in which the men in their lives worked. They would snicker, as if I were joking or being facetious. Their behavior reflected the way our society thinks, chooses its priorities, and allocates its resources. Unlike most Western-bloc countries, the United States does not provide a family or child allowance or some form of guaranteed income for all its citizens.[16] The United States also does not provide health care for all mothers and children as do most industrialized nations.

Major contradictions in our thinking and policies also contribute to the stigma and meager funding of welfare. Single mothers who are maintained by welfare benefits have been called "brood mares," "welfare madames," and other such negative epithets. In 1967, Russell Long, a U.S. senator from Louisiana, "publicly referred to welfare mothers as 'brood mares.' There was no sustained protest from leaders of either the women's movement or the civil rights movement."[17] The Reagan era brought "welfare madame" into public discourse. In stark contrast, married women who stay home and raise their children while depending on their husbands' income for economic support are valued because they fulfill the family ethic. The "family values" that were touted at the Republican National Convention in 1992 were based on such an ethic.

Mothers who are not dependent on a man, however, are not supposed to stay home and raise their children. They are expected to get job training and become self-supporting, to place their children in any kind of "day-care" they can find, and to care for the home and family alone after a full day's work. If as a result their children are injured, corrupted by drugs, or join street gangs, they are blamed for being bad mothers.[18] As observed by several students of the welfare system and our society's views of it, there is much classism and racism in the attitudes that prevail against women who depend on AFDC for a livelihood.[19] This helps to explain the contradictions inherent in our positive views of mothers who are economically dependent on husbands and our negative views of mothers who are economically dependent on the state.

Feminism, notes Theresa Funiciello, generally has not been supportive of mothers on welfare. This has added to the cultural stigma. In the early 1980s, feminism did take up the cause of the "displaced homemaker," the woman abandoned or divorced and left without income. But these concerns were directed at the women who had been affluent, not the poor or working-class women who constantly exist at the edge of poverty.[20] One mother on welfare responded to the women's liberation movement by writing that "freedom is not having to sell ass."[21] Her anger grew out of the fact that low benefits drive women living on AFDC to find whatever ways they can to survive. For some women, catering to the sexual needs of male companions who will bring groceries, loan cars, or buy clothes for the children is part of their survival tactics.

Neither has feminism been supportive of motherhood generally, although happily this has been changing over the last decade. A mother on AFDC found herself having to defend motherhood due to feminist denigration of women's traditional roles. She declared herself "in proud, open rebellion against a culture (including feminist culture) that devalues mothering."[22] She wrote: "I am not only rearing the next generation of society's workers, I am creating two new beings who will be fierce in their hatred of racism, sexism, and imperialism; and even fiercer in their love for humanity and justice. My mothering is part of a struggle for the future."[23] She adds that if there were not such contempt for motherhood, if mothers' worth were recognized, "single motherhood would not be nearly synonymous with poverty."[24]

Systemic Factors

Attitudes shape policies, and our society's negative attitudes about mothers sustained by AFDC, together with our general economic philosophies, have helped to formulate policies that are deliberately oppressive to women on welfare. AFDC benefits remain well below the poverty line in most states as a calculated incentive either to get women off public support or to get women to work outside the home to supplement their welfare income. The "official" rationale for keeping benefits low is the fear that if the entitlements were adequate to provide sufficient sustenance, then women would prefer being on welfare to seeking gainful employment.[25] The actual reason probably is related to the need of businesses for a pool of part-time, low-wage employees who can be exploited to keep our economic system running. This need has become more acute with lower birthrates over the last twenty-five years, restrictions on immigration, and tightening controls against illegal alien workers. The work provisions of recent welfare reforms are a way to meet the need for a larger population to capitalize on for our nation's economic well-being.[26] One woman has called welfare under the new reforms "death by exhaustion."[27]

State welfare policies also are structured in ways that, intentionally or not, inflict considerable harassment on the clients. The structure's inefficiencies make the whole experience negative and painful for most recipients. In some states a needy mother, pregnant or with baby in arms, may have to go to as many as nine different places, not all located under one roof or even in one part of the city, to receive the help to which she is entitled.[28] Cynical, overly cautious, or mean-spirited case workers also make the system harsh. As Ann Withorn points out, in many welfare agencies women are against women.[29] When I visited mothers who were entitled to more benefits than they were receiving, I would urge them to go back to the appropriate offices and push their causes further. Many would find excuses for not returning to what seemed to them like a battleground where they were destined to lose.[30]

Some forms of harassment are built into the system and are deliberate attempts to keep women receiving AFDC at constant risk. Earlier it was noted that welfare support is well below the official poverty level in most states. AFDC includes cash payments, rent subsidies, and food stamps as well as Medicaid and sometimes other programs. Yet housing needs are not necessarily covered by this system. In most areas the cash payments do not cover the average rent, and many landlords refuse to rent to people with housing subsidy certificates. The wait for government-subsidized housing is often a year.[31] Nutritional needs are just as difficult to meet. AFDC recipients say their monthly food stamps last an average of ten days.[32]

According to a group of women receiving AFDC, "the welfare system, in reality, has been set up to promote fraud as a means of survival. They *know* we can't live on budgets 'below the poverty line.' "[33] As explained in the foregoing discussion, some mothers on welfare survive with a string of male partners who help maintain their children in return for companionship and sexual favors. Yet women who are caught using this method of survival are considered fraudulent; and our society sees such behavior as promiscuity at best, government subsidized prostitution at worst. Other women work one or more low-paying jobs to survive. Yet the limits on their earnings are quite restrictive, and if they earn more than allowed, and report it, their welfare benefits are reduced.[34] If they fail to report it, they can be charged with fraud, taken to court, and in some cases banned from welfare. Even asking a friend or family member to give them money to help make ends meet at the end of the month is grounds for criminal charges and welfare denial if they do not report it as income.[35] All this is nothing less than entrapment. Mothers on welfare put it this way: "Like the wily fox, we are driven by hunger to the trap. We must carefully trip the trap, retrieve the bait, and escape, hopefully unscathed. Also similar to the fox, our incompetence can lead to starvation, disease, and death for ourselves and our families."[36] On the one hand, the AFDC benefits are so low that no one can survive on them. On the other hand, when women devise the best ways they can find to manage economically, they are considered criminals.

Because of these various forms of harassment and entrapment, women usually try to find ways to get off of welfare as soon as possible. When they succeed, it is often to the detriment of their own and their children's well-being. As already stated, few if any starting salaries for women will cover the many needs of growing children. Only recently have there been bridging programs, enabling women and their children to continue receiving food stamps, Medicaid, housing subsidies, and even adding day-care when they first return to marketplace employment. Yet these bridges usually are short lived, and due to low salaries some women have to return to full welfare assistance when the realities of their financial status add up to eviction, debt, untreated illnesses, or other long-term difficulties.[37]

The realities unveil a social crisis born of our nation's moral failings. Being a mother on welfare means being economically oppressed, socially stigmatized, and systematically harassed. It is a life that adds pain to the most difficult set of circumstances for single mothers and their children.

Thinking Ethically

The moral norms of womenviews provide alternative mirrors in which to assess the social crisis of oppressed, stigmatized, and harassed mothers on welfare. A norm of life-fostering creativity makes the work of mothering one of the most valuable labors of our society. The corresponding norm of transcending creativity leads to a different view of the "fraudulent" ways women devise in order to survive on welfare. An acceptance of dependence as the reality of being human not only presents those who are economically dependent on the state in more positive terms, but also points to the reality that those who care for dependent persons — be they children, persons with disabilities, or aging parents — are doing valuable work for our collective life. Cooperation and the power that arises from working together toward common goals of justice and mercy have special meaning for mothers on welfare who are reduced by the system to a basic survival mode and disempowered — indeed, dehumanized — by their status in life. The impact that each of these moral guidelines has on ethical thinking about mothers on welfare will be examined more fully in turn.

Transcending Creativity

A consistent norm of creatively giving and nurturing life, a norm such as the one expounded in chapter 2, places great value on the creative work women do in the home when they are bearing and rearing children. Stereotypes about what is valuable work must be overcome by both society at large and educated, middle-class feminists before the issue of what work is valuable can be resolved.[38] If mothering is seen as a socially valuable labor, this will alter our nation's perception of all women who work in the home while their children are young. As shown above, however, an appropriate valuing of motherhood is especially important for poor women who need welfare, because they are the ones who bear the heaviest burden of our present negative attitudes.

Our God-given ability to creatively transcend barriers to life also puts a different light on the diverse ways mothers on welfare cope with their deliberate impoverishment by the government. Clearly many of the ways that women find to survive on AFDC are illegal as the law is defined. But are women who practice fraud for their own and their children's survival immoral or is the system immoral? As already suggested, the system certainly is immoral. To knowingly put women in positions where they must find other means of support and then trap them when they turn to whatever means are available is unequivocally malevolent.

In all my years of working in homes and clinics with women on welfare, I never saw their scrambling for survival as anything but creative shrewdness, the human freedom to escape the ashes of despair, to affirm life, to deny death, to love self and others, to hate what oppressed them, to refuse to be treated as less than human. I learned from them an ethic of life affirmation, an ethic of transcending barriers to life.

Dependence

Dependence as the root reality of being human has profound implications for ethical thinking about mothers on welfare. Deuteronomy 15:4–11 says that there would be no poor if we shared the bounty that is available for humankind in the earth habitat that God has created for us. Yet because we are "hard-hearted," poverty always will exist and impoverished persons always will have to depend on society's assistance when times are especially bad. Families headed by single/abandoned/divorced women are a growing population of poor who must depend on our help. These women need economic maintenance that allows an acceptable life for themselves and their children, so that their important job of mothering can be accomplished. They need to be able to depend on our support because they are caring for the dependent ones among us — young children, handicapped children, elderly parents. We need their mothering labors because we depend on well-prepared citizens to support our democratic form of governance and keep our economy running. Mothers on welfare are providing important services for us, service on which we as a people depend, and yet we are afraid they will become "dependent" on the state. Our view of dependence is lopsided. We see only *their* dependence, not our own.

Cooperation

Some advocates for mothers on welfare are advising women to choose to depend on welfare assistance because they cannot depend on either men or the marketplace for economic survival.[39] But such advocates, many of whom have been recipients of AFDC, also advise women on welfare to become politically active for better economic and social foundations for themselves and their children. They balance economic dependence with the creative freedom to transcend barriers to life, and they see the importance of enabling cooperation among themselves. They cooperate in solidarity with all women suffering their plight. Such cooperative work for justice and mercy is empowering and helps mothers on welfare transcend barriers to their personhood as well as their own and their children's lives.[40]

Power

To respond morally to the crisis of welfare requires cooperative political and social action in solidarity *with* all women who are mothers. Reform of our welfare system cannot take place without an equal partnership between mothers on welfare and those with socioeconomic and sociopolitical power. To help accomplish this reform, those of us with such power must first find ways to empower mothers on welfare. One group has developed an inductive method for teaching both welfare recipients and feminist economists about the realities of the structural factors that promote and sustain the poverty of women. The purpose of this education is not job training but motivation for activism against the system.[41] We need mothers on welfare who are empowered in this or other effective ways. Only they can tell the story that allows us to feel their pain. Only they can help us see the realities of their situations. Only they can articulate truly just alternatives to the unjust system under which they now live. Yet they also need the help of people who are politically astute, whose voices are heard because of money or influence. Such help cannot be maternalistic or paternalistic. We must work in solidarity with mothers on welfare to change oppressive structures. We must be empowered by them to be adequate advocates who stand in solidarity with them for a just and merciful system.

Acting Morally

How should we as American Christians respond morally to the social crisis (perhaps it would be more apt to say "social disgrace") of mothers on welfare who are impoverished, stigmatized, and harassed? The foregoing discussion already has shown that America needs changes in policies and attitudes. Our political and social policies are denigrating not only to mothers on welfare in particular but also to mothers in general.

If we can change the way we see mothering and dependence, we will insist on a structure of need-adjusted economic support to all families with dependent children. This would phase out numerous other welfare programs and support services; and it would prevent the stigma now associated with AFDC. Supplementary support to two-parent families with dependent children also would allow low-income men to stay in relationships rather than depart so their families can receive state assistance. If combined with universal health coverage, a family supplement could have a major impact on reversing the dissolution of poor families in America. One advocate of such changes redefines work, showing that care-giving is every society's most precious labor and should be paid at minimum wages or above by the state. Also included in this vision of a more just world is a thirty-hour work week (six hours a day for five days), so both parents can share in outside jobs and still have time and energy to nurture children or other dependent persons in their families. Such a revised social structure would include day-care for persons of all ages who need supervision or custodial care.[42]

If the parenting and nurturing work that mothers do is appropriately valued, we also will wake up to the reality that all young people must be educated for care-giving work just as surely as they are educated for work in the marketplace. The job of caring for dependent children and adults, if valued sufficiently, will not be one segment of one elective class in one semester, but integrated into all required health and social studies courses beginning in elementary schools. Initially, educational preparation for care-giving should be extended to all families with preschool children until a whole generation has been taught that parenting is valuable and difficult work. Allowances or salaries for the work of parenting might be contingent on such classes.

All such educational efforts should be combined with the support and services needed for *adequate* care-giving. At the very least, these include not only fair payment for care-giving work, and subsidized day-care for all ages, but also affordable and available quality health services and safe housing; all must be in place before parents can do their jobs well. We have the economic wherewithal to accomplish this kind of social restructuring if we are willing to allocate our human and natural resources to life-affirming and nurturing approaches to our common life. Indeed, we cannot afford to do otherwise.

A system of economic maintenance that is adequate — above the poverty line with other services and supplements as required — will eliminate the necessity for mothers to work outside the home when their children are young. Note that I am saying "the *necessity* for mothers to work outside the home." For those women who prefer to work at jobs other than child care, we need economic supports and appropriate services to make their choice safe for their children and to protect their jobs and incomes when family responsibilities interrupt work schedules. We heard much from feminism in the 1960s and 1970s about liberating women from the home, and for many women this need is still crucial; but we live in a world where more and more women would like to be liberated from the economic necessity of a job that takes them out of the home when their children are young.

An appropriate level of support for mothers who are dependent solely on the state also would eliminate the need for some women to resort to fraud for survival. There always will be a few people who use fraudulent means to gain money — from state-supported persons to high-powered Wall Street brokers. Adequate economic backing and needed services for parenting will mean that fraud is something done by the immoral, not a way of survival for so many who are more moral than we who allow a system that entraps women trying to feed, house, and clothe their children.

7

REPRODUCTIVE CHOICES
Redefining the Issues

Feeling the Pain

"Every baby should be wanted," proclaimed an appealing poster of a baby taking off her shoes. This poster sat on tables and counters and hung on walls all over the health center as we launched a family planning initiative in the early 1970s. The image of the happy and wanted baby stood in sharp contrast to the lives of many of the abused and neglected children I encountered in my visits to homes of poor women burdened by too little money, too many mouths to feed, and insufficient abilities to manage the hard job of mothering, often without help from the children's fathers or grandparents.

One memory still sends shudders through my whole body every time I allow it to surface. In 1974 an AFDC social worker called and requested that I make a home visit to check the health of an eighteen-month-old boy. She said he was not progressing physically or mentally. When I arrived at the home, the mother, Dora, was expecting me. She came to the door with her three-year-old daughter, Kiesha, in tow. After introductions, I asked to see her son, Kevin. Dora did not go and fetch Kevin but pointed toward the bedroom where his crib stood. She did not accompany me to the room. The eighteen-month-old child lay still and stared blankly at the ceiling. He did not respond in any way to my presence. I noticed how thin his face was, but this did not prepare me for the shock of removing his blanket and seeing a starving child for the first time in my life. Malnourishment was common in the population I served, and many children probably went hungry at times. But this was like something we were to see later in the troubling television reports of starving children in Africa. Observations and probing questions, trademarks of public health nursing, riveted through my mind. Dora was tall, lanky, and probably slightly underweight; but she did not appear to be malnourished. Kiesha was well-developed physically, talkative, active — essentially a normal three-year-old on first glance. Why, then, was Kevin starving?

I reached across the railing, which would not lower, to pick up Kevin. Nothing in heaven or earth could have fortified me against the horror that I felt in that moment. Kevin's frail body was more rigid and less responsive than a plastic doll's. I realized in that instant that this baby had never been picked up, never been held. He did not know how to respond; indeed, he was not able to respond. To hold a living human being who seemed more inanimate than the dead babies I had carried to the morgue when I worked in pediatrics was painful beyond description. I wondered if my attempts to form his body to fit within a cradle in my arms was painful for him. He did not cry. He did not respond. Somehow I managed not to cry or scream at the mother or lose my ability to function in the role I was serving. I carried the baby to the living room and sat down to talk with Dora. My face must have said all that I was thinking and feeling and trying to hide. Tears ran down Dora's face.

"I didn't want him!" she blurted out, and she began to weep uncontrollably. Images of the poster and its caption wafted through my mind's eye: "Every baby should be wanted."

To allow time for both of us to regain our composure, I began performing a routine physical on Kevin. I listened to his heart and lungs. I examined him for birth defects or signs of abuse. I could not flex his arms or legs. He would not grip my fingers. He continued to be unresponsive in expression and bodily movement. Dora watched without questions, responding with minimal words to the questions I posed to her. I asked for a clean diaper and shirt for Kevin. Kiesha fetched them for me. I asked for a bottle to feed Kevin. Dora said he probably was not hungry, since he was not crying; but she brought what looked like skim milk.

Continuing to hold the baby, urging him to suck the bottle, hoping he finally would respond to food or human contact, I talked with the mother. I learned that she had never taken him to a doctor for a physical or immunizations; yet she took Kiesha regularly. She confirmed my conclusion that he had never been held. She changed his diapers once or twice a day; gave him a sponge bath occasionally; and propped his bottle on a rolled towel. He had never held the bottle, and she had not tried to feed him other foods. I asked about his eating schedule. She said she fed him when he cried, and that had become less and less frequently. Yesterday he had received two bottles. This was the first for today. It was nearly noon. I asked about the formula, and she said she used dry milk; her proportions were about half what they should have been.

Finally I asked the painful questions in as kindly a way as I could: "What happened? Why have you fed and cared for Kiesha and neglected Kevin?" Dora related her story to me with a mixture of anguish and anger. She wept and shouted. She wrung her hands and shook her fists.

Dora had been married when Kiesha was born. Her husband had been good to them and had provided an adequate though not ample livelihood.

When she told him she was pregnant with another child, he insisted that she get an abortion. He ranted and raved that he had not finished paying the hospital bill for Kiesha's birth, and he could not support any more children at that time. She told him it might be the boy he had hoped for when Kiesha was born. He said the boy would have to wait. She prayed for a miscarriage. She tried every folk remedy she knew to rid her body of the pregnancy. She starved herself. But she did not seek an abortion, which would have been illegal and, for poor women, unsafe at the time. Her mother had died when Dora was twelve years old due to a botched abortion; her only sister had been treated like a criminal when she was taken to the emergency room with profuse bleeding after an illegal abortion. Now her sister could not have any children.

She told me that she had hated the baby more and more as each month of the pregnancy passed and her husband withdrew. When Kevin was born, and her husband left the day she and the baby were discharged from the hospital, she could not bear even to care for the baby. When his cries became too persistent, she would change him and prop a bottle so she could forget he was there.

I wondered if she had thought about adoption, but I did not ask her. I did ask her about siblings or aunts or cousins who might have taken care of Kevin. She said she had tried this, but all of them had to work outside the home. I did not ask her if she was hoping the baby would die; the answer was obvious.

Both children were removed from the home. It was an action I could understand with my head, but my heart was wrenched by the mother's pain at losing the child she loved. Kevin gradually responded to good foster care, but brain and personality damage were so great that he will always live with severe limitations. I do not know what happened to Dora or Kiesha, but I continue to be haunted by my memory of them. Most haunting of all is the realization that in 1973, the same year Dora gave birth to her unwanted son, elective abortion was legalized and funded by public clinics so that women of every economic level had access to medically safe abortions.

Dora's treatment of Kevin was extreme, although many unwanted babies are neglected or abused. Her situation in relation to the baby's father and family income, however, was typical. In my memories of public health nursing, the economic stresses of families faced with unplanned pregnancies or unwanted babies are writ large. My experience suggests that if Dora's husband had not been solely responsible for another baby, he probably would not have abandoned the family. More and more as I reflect on my encounters with families where children were unwanted, neglected, and abused, I realize that "Every baby should be wanted" is not just a personal or family matter. Wanted babies are a matter for all of us. If the larger community into which babies are born were willing to support them, then less babies would be unwanted before birth or neglected and abused after birth.

Seeing the Realities

As I drafted this chapter in the summer of 1992, the whole nation was assessing recent Supreme Court rulings on the question of abortion. On the one hand, a slim majority (five to four) not only upheld *Roe v. Wade* but grounded it more firmly in constitutional guarantees of freedom for self-determination. On the other hand, a decided majority (seven to two) upheld states' rights to control circumstances surrounding abortions in ways that for many women will limit their freedom to exercise their rights to reproductive self-determination. Subsequent decisions have supported both rulings.

Despite the legal status of abortion, however, medically safe legal abortions are increasingly unavailable to large segments of the population due to politically motivated obstacles to access. Many women have to travel hundreds of miles for medically safe abortions because so few physicians are willing to perform them that 83 percent of this nation's counties do not have an identified abortion provider.[1] *Time* magazine reports that physicians who are willing to perform abortions often travel hundreds of miles to cover areas where no local physicians dare to perform the procedure due to threats to their families and staffs by antiabortion terrorists. *Time* also cites evidence that physicians who try to locate in poor or working-class neighborhoods and risk a practice that includes abortion are harassed by public officials so that they cannot set up the necessary equipment. Women seeking abortions encounter further barriers in states that legislate counseling, consent or notification stipulations, waiting periods, and other restrictions that for teenage and poor women could delay abortions beyond the first trimester, when they are safest. State financial support for abortions is sporadic, so many women cannot afford the procedure even if it is available to them. Barrier-creating states far outnumber the states that intend to keep abortion legal and financially accessible.[2]

As I finalize this chapter early in 1993, America awaits the impact of a newly inaugurated President Clinton. Clinton has declared himself openly pro-choice (but not pro-abortion) and already has used executive powers to assure wider compliance to the law of *Roe v. Wade*. Only time will show whether such actions in the White House will in fact change the reality for all women. At present, restrictions that hamper elective choices for abortion together with lack of affordable or even available abortions in many localities mean that poor and working-class women are being denied a procedure that financially more fortunate women can obtain, often without hassle. Thus women without access to medically safe abortions increasingly seek illegal alternatives that endanger their lives.[3]

If we have reached a point where only women with adequate money can obtain medically safe abortions, then *Roe v. Wade* already has been abolished in effect even if not by judiciary fiat. Regardless of the law, women with money have been able to buy medically safe abortions ever since they became available. They always will.

As asserted above, abortion is a sociopolitical and socioeconomic matter, not merely a personal moral decision. Yet much of the abortion debate, whether in the courts or in the streets or in the church or in the scholarly guild, seems to swirl around a full or empty womb abstracted not only from the woman as a person but also from the society as a community of support for new life in its midst.[4] Ethicists and clergy, who are predominantly male, have centered their moral concerns on whether or when the product of conception is fully human before birth. While focusing on such questions that can be answered only in theory, for the most part they have ignored the actual human context in which pregnancies occur and into which babies are born.[5]

To be considered here are four social and personal realities that have an impact on the abortion question but are not often heard in the debate. First, a few historical insights about unwanted pregnancies will be contemplated. These provide a context in which to examine pertinent contraceptive, relational, and societal realities that must be understood in order to make a reasoned response to the impassioned abortion issue.

Historical Realities

When our contemporary situation is seen in historical context, some realism is brought to abortion dialogue. Abortion, infanticide, abandonment, and placement have been practiced in Western/Christian culture since its beginning. In preindustrial Europe, during hard economic times, infanticide was so prevalent that corpses of newborns littered streets and swelled trash heaps.[6] America has not been exempt from such practices, but due to our land and economic expansion capabilities, we usually have been able to support children. According to Susan Power Bratton, Christian churches in preindustrial Europe looked the other way when the economy was weak and infanticide was widely practiced, although many babies were placed in monasteries and convents (or abandoned at their gates); and when the number of unwanted children became too great the church built inhumane foundling hospitals.[7] The media exposed the reality that history repeats itself. In Romania under Communist rule, abortion was illegal and women were coerced to bear children they could not care for. Consequently, vast numbers of unwanted babies were warehoused in inhumane conditions.[8] Studies show that in the past and the present, in cultures around the globe, when conditions are good children are welcomed as a blessing, especially in agricultural and industrial areas; but when conditions are threatening to existence, children are abandoned or disposed of when they become burdens.[9]

Today in America, dead infants continue to be discovered in the garbage, and abandoned babies are found in numerous places. The numbers are less than they might be, however, because many women can obtain abortions to rid their bodies and our collective lives of unwanted new life among us. A brief look at just some of the realities that lead to so many unwanted pregnancies will contribute more clarity to the moral issues around abortion.

Contraceptive Realities

Unwanted pregnancies may be the result of rape or incest; they may have occurred because of unprotected sex; they may be caused by improper use of contraceptives; or they may be due to new medical technologies that allow parents to know whether a baby will have a congenital disease or be severely malformed or otherwise unable to live a normal life.[10] But a large number of abortions are sought due to unplanned pregnancies that occur in spite of careful use of contraceptives for prevention.

One study estimates that as many as 90 percent of abortions would be eliminated if effective contraceptives were available and used properly.[11] In other words, in the ideal world, we still would have at least 10 percent as many unwanted pregnancies as we have today. In the real world, approximately 10 percent of women using contraceptives have unplanned pregnancies. Few people are aware of the high percentage of failure even with the careful use of contraceptives. According to a 1980s study, contraceptive failure was 4 to 10 percent for the combined hormone pill, 5 percent for the IUD (intrauterine device), 5 percent for condoms with spermicides, 10 percent for condoms alone, 17 percent for the diaphragm with spermicide, and 20 to 25 percent for spermicides alone.[12] Newer and longer-lasting hormonal preparations are being used now and promise more protection than the pill, but the fact is that some women cannot tolerate any of the hormonal contraceptives, due to health problems that are exacerbated by their use. The IUD has caused so many difficulties that few physicians recommend it anymore. Thus many women cannot use two of the most effective methods of contraception. Because of these problems for certain women, one church member who works at Planned Parenthood said that for some couples, the only safe contraceptive other than sterilization is two-barrier methods plus the willingness to have a first-trimester abortion.

Another matter that often is neglected in the abortion debate is the expense of contraceptives. Even though they cost less than the alternatives, tight budgets could mean failure to have prescriptions filled or to purchase over-the-counter methods. For more and more women on limited or insufficient incomes, necessities for today take budgetary precedence over an unknown future. Thus, for some women negligence in the use of contraceptives may be caused by economic factors.

Despite these several realities about contraceptives, some church position papers continue to place unwarranted faith in contraceptive technologies and women's access to them. They uphold freedom of choice for women, but they also say that abortion should not be used for family planning purposes. Some antiabortion church positions also seem to ignore or distort contraceptive failure as a reason for a large percentage of abortions.

The matter of contraceptives is even more complicated by the fact that some of the most influential voices against abortion are also against contraception. Other abortion foes accept or even promote contraception for mature, preferably married, women but do not want knowledge or possession of contraceptives to be made available to young people. In today's culture, such attitudes are self-defeating. European nations that have both legal and readily available elective abortions, and realistic policies of teaching human sexuality in the schools and making contraceptives available for young people, have much lower abortion rates than the United States.[13]

Relational Realities

A second and even more important reality of life that is ignored or slighted in the abortion debate comes from women's ways of thinking and acting morally. Psychologists are finding increasing evidence that women make moral decisions on the basis of interpersonal connections rather than on the basis of abstract moral norms. In her ground-breaking study of women choosing whether or not to have abortions, Carol Gilligan found that "women identified repeatedly the moral problem as a problem of *responsibility*. If one is to be responsible for having a child, one has to ask, Is it possible to care for this child?"[14] Yet Gilligan also found that women's moral decision making about abortion did not stop with concern for the care of the one to be born, but extended to themselves and their relational commitments. She found that "women searched for an inclusive solution, for a way to avoid harm both to others *and* to themselves." If such solutions were not found, then the women "tended to ask which alternative would do the least harm" to all concerned.[15] Such studies suggest that women are socialized to a female way of making moral decisions — focused on responsibility for the unborn, the self, and all relevant relationships.

My own experiences with four pregnancies, and the emotions and sensations reported by the many mothers I served as a nurse, suggest a further consideration of moral decision making on the question of abortion. Even though women have a sense of responsibility toward their future babies, few begin to develop a *relationship* with the unborn until well into the second trimester, when quickening occurs. Quickening, the first movement of the fetus felt by the mother, is like holding a baby bird in one's hands and sensing just the slightest timid flutter of wings. Before quickening, women sense changes in their own bodies. They may know intellectually that a new being is growing, but they do not *feel* the baby as separate from themselves. As the fetus grows and moves and kicks, most women begin to bond with the future child they will bear. Yet the kind of bonding that fosters human relationships does not begin to take place until after birth, when parents and babies experience direct responses to their interactions.[16] Thus, when women contemplate abortion in the first trimester of a pregnancy, the unborn may not be primary among the relationships to be weighed and balanced.

Given these realities of women's decision-making approaches and their experiences of pregnancy, they may end unwanted pregnancies because they do not believe they can be responsible to a potential relationship and still fulfill commitments to already established relationships. Or women may believe it is morally wrong to bring new life into relationships or a world that would prevent them from caring for the child in ways that are responsible.

Such relationally derived and emotionally fostered decisions do not conform to the kind of abstract and absolute ethical norms about sanctity of life or murder prohibitions that abound in moral dictates against abortion. We have been taught to think in abstract and objective terms about moral issues. We have believed that individuals or the church or the courts, by unemotional appeals to absolute philosophical ideals or theological beliefs, could determine whether something was right or wrong, good or evil. Instead, women have been found to base moral decisions on personal commitments. Confusion and rancor result from failure to realize that the way moral decisions are made by women contemplating abortion is very different from the way most religionists, legislators, and judges think about the issue. Although most women are informed about our culture's abstract norms, their moral choices for or against continuing pregnancies are based more often on responsibility to the unborn, themselves, or existing relationships than on abstract ethical codes or laws.

Societal Realities

When women ask whether or not they can take care of a baby, the circumstances that help them make what Beverly Wildung Harrison rightly calls a moral choice for abortion[17] extend beyond individuals and families. In the chapter on welfare, I discussed studies that showed that more and more women are finding themselves in very tenuous relationships with their male partners and with the larger community. Women cannot depend on the fathers of their children to help care for babies economically or in other ways. They cannot rely on America's societal structures to provide them with adequate economic support or other services to help in the raising of their children. Awareness that they cannot depend on others or society to help them with a pregnancy and the care of a new life may lead many women to choose abortion as the most responsible way to deal with an unplanned and unwanted pregnancy.

Such realities are not considered by many staunch antiabortionists. The *New York Times* reports that members of the National Right to Life Political Action Committee "say they really do not care much about...other issues, including the economy, education, jobs and health care." The PAC's director, Carol Long, declared that "stopping abortion is such a big part of my life that nothing else is important."[18] Statements of this temper reflect a contradiction that abortion foes simply will not see. This contradiction was evident when New Jersey's leading newspaper published a long article entitled "Quiet Cries," with a picture of the grim reaper walking through a field of children and a caption reading: "Statistics show children are receiving inadequate health care, following decade of drastic cuts in federal aid to nation's cities." The article reported that because low-income mothers do not receive prenatal care, forty thousand infants die annually in the United Sates.[19] Disproportionate numbers of impoverished U.S. children also die of conditions or diseases that are curable or preventable with healthy living conditions, good nutrition, medical care, and vaccines.[20] Antiabortion forces choose to be blind to the socioeconomic realities of our common life that place vast numbers of women in the position of feeling that abortion is their only moral option when an unplanned pregnancy occurs.

Despite the so-called pro-life rhetoric of the abortion-opposing leadership over the last decade or more, our nation has become increasingly antilife for all citizens, but especially for women and children.[21] In contrast, many industrialized nations are decidedly pro-life in their social and economic supports for women's work of bearing and rearing children; at the same time these nations protect elective abortion as a health care option. Some of the social structures that make a society truly pro-life are health care, day-care, family leaves that do not jeopardize employment, family allowances, and a generally strong economy that promises a livelihood not only for this generation but also the next. These economic and social supports are not guaranteed for most Americans.

Increasing numbers of American women of childbearing age have no health insurance. Many people erroneously believe that working people have insurance, and unemployed people have Medicaid. But approximately 70 percent of the current thirty-six million uninsured people either work in jobs that do not include health insurance benefits or are denied coverage due to chronic illnesses or catastrophic diseases.[22] Medicaid covers only 40 percent of the poor. Furthermore, despite federally mandated expansion of Medicaid for the coverage of children, recent economic downturns have forced many states to narrow the windows of eligibility or the range of benefits.[23] Women who do have Medicaid, however, have a difficult time finding an obstetrician or pediatrician who will accept the reduced payments the program offers; they are forced to use publicly run clinics if any are available in their areas. In addition to uninsured families, another twenty million Americans are underinsured, meaning their coverage is inadequate to meet their health care needs.[24] As unions lose their power in a belt-tightening economy, more and more insured workers find their coverage so minimal that costs for even a normal labor and delivery, with all the attendant care to mother and baby, are covered at 50 percent or less. Moreover, the growing litigation against obstetricians is causing the pool of available ones to shrink, and this raises prices so that even insured patients and their insurers have higher costs.

A medically safe abortion is never as expensive as a birth, to say nothing of ongoing maternal and child health needs. As stated earlier, the need for health care was a major factor in women's decisions to leave low-paying jobs and live on welfare support. The lack of health insurance coverage or adequate health services is also a major reason for seeking an abortion, not only for impoverished women, but for increasing numbers of women in the working and middle classes.

American women recognize the shaky ground they occupy in relation to men and the social structures. Thus more and more women today prepare to be self-supporting. How do unplanned pregnancies fit into such a world? The dilemma women face when they have an unplanned pregnancy and their income is needed for family support is staggering. Meanwhile, neither our government nor our business community is providing economically secure circumstances for women to carry and raise children, even within marriages. Paycheck tax deductions for dependents and year-end deductions for health expenses and day-care costs are not sufficient to enable low- to middle-income families to provide for children in today's economy. Such families need more financial assistance than present tax structures provide; and they also need either the money or subsidized services in advance, since most have no reserves to draw upon.

America's eroding education system is another deterrent to the bringing forth of children, especially in depressed urban areas and many rural locations. Growing numbers of poor and middle-class people feel the present situation in many of our public schools makes bringing children into the world less and less appealing. Many parents do not want to have children until they have the financial ability either to move to areas where schools are safer and more effective or to pay tuition for private or parochial schools. A working couple faced with an unplanned pregnancy while trying to get on firmer financial ground may choose abortion out of concern for their future offspring.

Despite our advances in many facets of life, we are not so different from people throughout human history who have killed infants or abandoned unwanted children in hard times. Unless we have a strong economy and enough jobs to keep wages and benefits up, children are economic burdens that neither families nor society can bear. Until we have social and economic supports for bearing and rearing children, many pregnancies will be terminated by abortions, whether or not they are legal. Those who want to reduce the incidences of abortion might well look at the realities that cause women to choose abortion and then realign their priorities to make the entire social system supportive of life.[25]

Thinking Ethically

Womenviews of human life, as worked out in part 1, provide particular mirrors in which to reflect ethically on issues around abortion. These mirrors have shaped all of the discussion on the matter thus far, but here the norms and values are lifted up more explicitly. Womenviews inform moral perspectives in ways that are consistent with women's lived realities as childbearers.

Transcending Creativity

An ethic of life, based on our creating and transcending freedom to give and sustain life, might lead to the assumption that womenviews would be totally against abortion. If human procreativity is abstracted from the context of other lived realities, abortion would seem to be a repudiation of life. But the norm of transcending creativity specifically negates the idea that women's creative work is only the bringing forth of new life. Transcending creativity is seen as the freedom for engendering both life and a life-sustaining world — in other words, the freedom for survival. The first can never be separated from the second; nor should it necessarily compromise the second. Therefore, a norm of life-fostering transcending and creating freedom, understood in terms of our God-given gifts for survival, does not lead necessarily to a moral prohibition of abortion.

This matter of survival takes on wider moral connotations in the context of ecological concerns. Sallie McFague argues that "siding with life as such is not 'pro-life' in the sense of being antiabortion." McFague's ethic of life is "concerned with the nurture and fulfillment of life, not just with birth." In addition, the pro-life ethic she has worked out in thinking of God as mother is concerned with all species, and unlimited human growth can deprive other species of their habitats.[26] Bratton shows that children born in industrial democracies, where disproportionate percentages of natural and economic resources are consumed, deprive people of life in other parts of the world.[27] When the interdependence of all people and our utter dependence on this planet are recognized, one individual life in the womb of one particular woman takes on very different moral dimensions.

Dependence

As seen in the previous chapter, the radical reality of human dependence has societal implications. Some of the lived realities that lead women to choose abortion, which were discussed above, remind us of the newborn's utter dependence on us. "Us" is not the mother, or both parents, or the extended family; "us" is the whole community of living beings who depend on one another and habitat earth for survival. New life depends on a society that is willing and able to make the necessary investment of resources and services to support women and children. "Every baby should be wanted" enough by the whole society that provisions are made for women and children to have a good life.

Sidney Callahan represents a decidedly feminist and antiabortion stance on this matter. She argues that when women choose abortion they release fathers and the larger society from the responsibility to care for dependent children. She believes this perpetuates the present neglect of childbearing and child-rearing needs.[28] Her argument offers an important alternative to voices on both sides of the abortion divide. Yet Callahan's perspective is problematic. She ignores the fact that an antiabortion stance is not the same as a pro-life position. Several European nations whose laws protect elective abortions illustrate that a society can be pro-life in the sense of supporting childbearing and the rearing of dependent children. Furthermore, if women holding to such views want a society that both affirms motherhood and cares for dependent children, they should work toward having the social and economic supports in place before they expect couples or single mothers to opt for birth. Otherwise, for the sake of systemic change, these antiabortion women are exacting an unjust price from many parents and/or their offspring.

Cooperation

Women really do need to cooperate on this issue of abortion, and I use the term "cooperate" in the sense of being co-workers with God for a just and merciful world. Historically, men have both protected their myth of reproductive superiority and feared women's larger reproductive roles; this has led to attempts to control and coerce women's procreative powers.[29] Despite present knowledge about reproductive science, and much awareness about women's larger role in reproduction of the species, the continuing male dominance in the medical sciences, the legislatures, and the courts means that men still are in situations to control women's reproductive creativity in ways that may not be beneficial to women and children. Women need to draw on their own experiences and perceptions in order to work together for moral ways of thinking and acting in relation to this troubling question of abortion.

Power

An ethic of life-affirming and transcending creativity, which is in tension with human dependence and in need of justice-promoting cooperation, can be exercised by women only if they have power to make moral choices autonomously. Such power cannot exist without guaranteed rights of self-determination. As I write, the law of the land protects women's rights of self-determination, which necessarily include the right to choose abortion. This right cannot be denied women in any state or territory of the United States. Women's need for legal power in relation to abortion is seen as unique because of women's particular role in reproduction. The Supreme Court opinion of June 1992 that reaffirmed this power argued that

> these matters [of reproduction], involving the most intimate and personal choices a person may make in a lifetime, choices central to personal dignity and autonomy, are central to the liberty protected by the Fourteenth Amendment. At the heart of liberty is the right to define one's own concept of existence, of meaning, of the universe, and of the mystery of human life.[30]

The court has granted most adult women the power to make a *unilateral* decision to have an abortion for personal, family, or societal reasons.

Clearly, women do need politically guaranteed rights to make reproductive choices. Yet moral reflection on women's realities calls into question some of the rhetoric about rights that has been heard in the abortion debate. The concept of rights that pervades our lives came out of the Enlightenment that fostered the American and French revolutions of the eighteenth century. Rights, believed to be based in some ultimate reality, are in fact realized only when a community guarantees them as part of its covenant with one another. Our tradition, however, has never held rights to be as autonomous as we hear today in many areas of life. Politically guaranteed rights always have been balanced by or in tension with the rights of others.

Such a view of rights is contrary to much rhetoric on both sides of the abortion divide. To argue, as do many foes of abortion rights, that the unborn have rights that are not contingent on the rights of the parent(s) or the family or the community or the habitat into which that new life will come and be dependent upon for its care is a major distortion of rights thinking.[31] To hold, as many abortion-rights advocates do, that women have rights to do whatever they please with their bodies is equally problematic from a moral perspective. Furthermore, no thinking woman would be willing to grant men that same right.

Prevailing views of rights also cannot be equated with morality. A decision based on the exercise of a right does not have the same moral standing as a decision rooted in a sense of responsibility for life and relationships.[32] Court-defined legal rights must be distinguished from women-defined moral choices. The legal right is necessary for women to have full power for self-determination, but women do not make *moral* choices about abortion because it is their right. Rather, their right gives them the freedom to make moral choices. Women are thereby empowered by the court to be fully human.

Acting Morally

As asserted in the preceding discussion, an ethic of transcending creativity for life, particularly when held in tension with the reality of dependence and the empowerment of cooperative efforts, does not necessarily preclude abortion. Nevertheless, the imperative to create life in all its richness and to transcend barriers to that life does compel a moral response that is decidedly pro-life in the context of justice and mercy. In the previous chapter evidence was presented to show that our socioeconomic systems require major restructuring if we are to fulfill such a moral destiny. If we cooperated to change our socioeconomic structures so they would support human life — women, children, and families — then we could claim to be a truly pro-life people.

As already indicated, to be truly pro-life, our society should be one in which women can depend on the scientific community to provide safe and effective contraceptives for both sexes. A pro-life society also must include healthy childbearing and child rearing, which are dependent on adequate health services. We fail to realize that unless we cooperate as a nation to provide effective and available contraceptives and universal health care (including abortions) to all citizens we are not co-working with God for a world that sustains life. To raise children in today's world also requires realistic family allowances, job-secure family leaves, safe and affordable day-care, effective free schools in all communities, and an economy that guarantees not only the parents but the next generation a means to earn a livelihood. Reasonable measures of success in such efforts would reduce the number of unplanned pregnancies and might offer many women the opportunity to exercise their powers of reproductive freedom to choose birth as the more responsible moral act.

8

ADDICTION
Renaming the Problem

Feeling the Pain

The unpainted, dilapidated frame house sat next to the railroad tracks in an industrial area of the city. Inside, a wood stove dominated a small living room, where I sat talking with Mabel. The house was cold on that late fall morning, and there was no wood for the fire. With winter approaching rapidly, Mabel did not know how she was going to heat the house. Her husband was out of work, and she was feeling too poorly to work.

I was there to provide prenatal teaching to Mabel, who was halfway through her sixth pregnancy. She had two living children, Elaine, who was ten, and Jimmy, who was eight. Two babies had been premature and died in infancy. Mabel had delivered a stillborn baby at home just over a year ago.

Elaine came in the back door through the kitchen, which drew my attention in that direction. Beer cans literally filled the room — on every counter and table, in the sink, on the floor, in bags. Since my son made extra money by finding aluminum cans on the beach and taking them to a recycling center, I first assumed this was the reason for the massive collection. I asked Elaine if she and her brother were earning money this way; she told me her mother and daddy drank all the beer. Mabel looked sheepish. I did not know how to respond, so I focused on other matters to escape my sense of inadequacy to deal with the drinking problem. I was afraid that addressing her alcohol consumption would close the door to the reasons I had made the visit.

I asked Elaine why she was home, since it was a school day. Mabel answered: "She's sick." After further questions and a brief physical examination, I suspected that Elaine had a severe case of rheumatic fever with heart involvement. I gave Mabel an appointment card to bring Elaine to the children's clinic the next day.

I next turned my attention to Mabel and her pregnancy. I took her blood pressure, which had been high at her last clinic visit. We talked about nutrition, her feelings about this pregnancy after the loss of three babies, her plans for this baby, and community assistance that she could get for health services, family planning, money, food, and transportation. Finally I dared to talk with her about the beer.

She was surprisingly honest about the level of her consumption. She said she and her husband had been drinking beer every night since they were married. At the time, health care providers were not widely aware of the extensive adverse effects of alcohol on the fetus, so I concentrated my concerns on whether she would be able to take care of herself and the baby if she drank so much. I talked about the cost when there was insufficient money for food and fuel. She admitted that this was a problem.

When Mabel did not bring Elaine to the clinic the next day, I returned to the home. This time my visit was in the late afternoon. Both Mabel and her husband, Tom, were present and drunk. Elaine and Jimmy were "out playing." It was a cold, rainy day, and the house felt like a refrigerator. I hoped the children were at a neighbor's where there were warmth and sobriety. I asked why Elaine had not been brought to the clinic. Mabel said she did not have the money for bus fare. I was prepared with arrangements for free transportation. The next day, when the driver went to pick up Mabel and Elaine for the clinic appointment, no one answered the door.

Over the next several months, even with the intervention of social services, all attempts to get Mabel to bring Elaine to the clinic failed. Mabel attended only one more prenatal appointment before her baby boy was born. With the help of other community services the family managed to obtain food stamps and supplements from food pantries when needed. And somehow wood was found for the stove. The drinking, however, was not addressed.

The baby survived because of Elaine's care, even though she was too sick to go to school. After several more months, social services finally intervened, removed Elaine from the home, and got her the medical attention she needed for her rheumatic fever and many complications that had developed over the years of neglect. She was hospitalized for six months. Jimmy stayed home from school to care for the baby on days when his mother did not get up in the morning. Mabel and Tom continued to drink even though they were warned that the other two children would be removed from the home if Jimmy did not attend school regularly and the baby was not taken to the clinic as scheduled.

Even without the additional and considerable impairment caused by the parents' drug addiction, this family had limited abilities to cope with life and manage a home. Both Mabel and Tom had only grade-school education, and Mabel appeared to be slightly retarded, whether congenitally or because of brain damage from alcoholism, I could not tell. Almost five years earlier, the family had emigrated from a rural area of another state to the city where I worked. Their expectations of better financial fortunes had not proved realistic, since they had no job skills.

Alcohol addiction of mothers, fathers, and even teenagers was not un-common in my public health work. Illegal drug use also was prevalent, although not openly. And health problems related to tobacco addiction took up a considerable amount of my time. Yet this family's tragic situation has continued to trouble me because it occurred early in my public health work and I was not yet aware of how impaired a family could become with excessive consumption of beer. I did not see then, as I do now, the relationship between the premature and dead babies and the mother's alcoholism. I did not accept the reality that kept Mabel from bringing Elaine to the clinic; I saw her as simply irresponsible. I did not understand or know how to address the family's primary problem: addiction.

Seeing the Realities

"Addiction" has become a buzzword in some psychological, philosophical, and sociological circles. The word "addiction" is being used by some people in these several disciplines to get a handle on what they believe is wrong with this world: unhealthy norms, values, perceptions, and behaviors that lead to all the problems this society faces. This point of view has been embraced and popularized most sweepingly by Anne Wilson Schaef, whose feminist-psychological perspective leads her to label most individuals and every institution as addicted. While her definitions of addiction are multifarious, one core definition is that "an addiction is any process over which we are powerless."[1] Equally important in her understanding of addiction is what she sees as an almost universal condition of human beings today: choosing neither to live nor to die, but existing like zombies in a meaningless world.[2] According to Schaef, all other behaviors exhibited by addicted persons and institutions occur in support of these primary problems.

Such an all-inclusive definition of addiction obscures the reality of one of its most devastating forms — chemical impairment. Defining addiction in such sweeping terms also paralyzes us as a society when we try to address the particular addictions to chemicals that impair individuals, families, and whole communities to such obvious degrees. In this chapter, I narrow the focus to chemical addictions.

Drugs — and I mean by the term both legal and illegal addictive substances that are inhaled, ingested, and injected — are used by people of every race and color, of every socioeconomic status, in urban, suburban, and rural areas. Despite media portrayals of drug use as primarily an urban ghetto problem, potentially addicting drugs are used in all socio-demographic communities in the United States, which is "the world's largest drug consumer."[3] Psychological or physical pain and other "uncomfortable life situations, such as boredom, loneliness, frustration, fear, low self-esteem, and changing life styles and roles," are some of the reasons people turn to drugs.[4] Some seek escape — anesthesia or amnesia; some seek pleasure — euphoria or relaxation; some seek a fix — enhanced abilities to manage their world that seems unmanageable when they are sober. Most come from dysfunctional families or dysfunctional communities or both.[5] For physical or psychological reasons, some persons who turn to drugs for any of these reasons become addicted and without help cannot escape the hold the chemicals have on their bodies and their lives. Their addictions have widespread socioeconomic and sociopolitical ramifications that have led to a social crisis of enormous dimensions.

The drug crisis is far too broad and complex to cover in one chapter, and this section can focus on just one aspect of the realities surrounding the crisis: our nation's inappropriate responses to chemical addictions in poor minority populations. These realities can be called "women's abuse," "class and race abuse," and "national abuse." These realities are more sociopolitical and socioeconomic than personal or psychological.

Women's Abuse

Women of all cultures, races, and economic status are at high risk for drug impairment because of low self-esteem.[6] Women who have access to the health care system frequently are overtreated or wrongly treated with tranquilizers, sedatives, and other emotionally and physically addictive substances.[7] Many such women have multiple addictions, combining nicotine, alcohol, one or more prescriptions, over-the-counter medication, and sometimes one or more illegal drugs. Women who do not have economic access to prescription drugs still may have multiple addictions to legal as well as illegal substances.[8]

According to Jean Searjeant Watt, chemical addictions of women often are hidden because women are more likely than men to use drugs primarily in the home and are less likely to join a therapy group or go to a treatment center. Watt observes that women who are addicted suffer from negative cultural biases based on a double standard. On the one hand, these biases hold that women are supposed to be the purer, more moral, sex that does not use drugs; on the other hand, when women are chemically impaired, these biases lead to the belief that women behave less responsibly than men with the same addictions. Chemically impaired women find this virgin/whore dichotomy, which all women are expected to negotiate in patriarchal societies, to be a deterrent to admitting their addiction problems and seeking help.[9]

One urban study revealed several important factors contributing to black and white women's use of addictive drugs. Examining women's use of alcohol in Baltimore, three public health researchers found that black women were "at no greater risk than whites for heavy drinking or for suffering from alcohol abuse or dependence."[10] The same study showed that women of both races who had not completed high school drank more heavily than women with high school or higher levels of education. Among educated women, however, more white than black women were heavy drinkers.[11] Women of both races who had annual incomes below six thousand dollars drank more than women with higher incomes.[12] This study provides two important insights: first, that racial and ethnic stereotypes that assume people of color are more inclined to addictions seem to be erroneous; second, that inadequate education, lack of job skills, and low income — all of which can lead to or come from poor self-esteem — appear to be among the causes of alcohol addiction in urban women.

Because of women's childbearing capabilities, their addiction generates particular problems. Drug addiction of pregnant women is causing one of society's most heartrending crises. One study showed that 10 percent of the babies born in the United States are affected by their mothers' cocaine or other illegal drug use. In New York City, "the incidence of maternal substance abuse recorded in birth certificates ... tripled between 1981 and 1987." In Los Angeles County, during a three-year period, fetal deaths related to maternal use of drugs rose from nine to fifty-six. Increasingly, the response to drug-addicted newborns has been to treat their mothers as criminals. Drug use during pregnancy is equated with child abuse.[13]

This trend to prosecute and incarcerate drug-impaired mothers has occurred at the same time that drug treatment facilities routinely have denied treatment to women who were pregnant. Jacqueline Berrien reports that even though there is awareness of the increase in "maternal drug use and drug-exposed infants," no corresponding increase has occurred "in the number of drug treatment facilities for pregnant women." In New York City, for example, less than half of the existing drug treatment centers will accept any pregnant women, and only about 10 percent will accept crack-addicted pregnant women who have Medicaid. In addition, "only two of 87 drug treatment programs in the city furnished child care for their patients who were parents." For rural women, the situation is even worse, since treatment centers are so sparse in remote areas.[14]

Many addicted mothers are young and poor minority women, victimized by racism and classism; yet drug addiction among pregnant women is not confined to this sociodemographic group. Nevertheless, often "government programs for detecting drug exposure in infants ... target women who rely upon public facilities," in other words, largely impoverished minority women. Furthermore, racism and classism exist in the different assumptions health providers have about their patients. Women who use public facilities for health care are tested for drugs routinely, whereas women who use private health services usually are not tested. And women are tested for only illegal drugs during pregnancy, not for tobacco and alcohol, which have been shown to damage the fetus.

Sexism also is evident, as women are singled out for both testing and criminal prosecution, while men are not. Men are not held responsible for secondhand cigarette smoke that might damage a fetus; nor have men "been required to avoid exposure to drugs or chemicals known to cause damage to the sperm." And if a fetus is injured due to woman-battering by a drug-affected male partner, he probably will not be prosecuted.[15] Racism, classism, and sexism combine to generate double standards that affect women addicted to drugs.

From the perspectives of many impoverished women who are addicted, this country's "war on drugs" seems to have its guns aimed at mothers who use illegal drugs during their pregnancies. There is only minimal commitment to treatment of drug-impaired pregnant women to prevent them from killing their unborn or giving birth to drug-damaged or drug-addicted babies. They are treated like child abusers if they cannot stop using the drugs on their own, even though therapists claim that this is almost impossible to do.

Class and Race Abuse

Pregnant women are not the only drug users whose addiction is being treated as a crime and not a disease. Those in inner cities who turn to illegal drugs to escape the reality of "no exit" — and this encompasses large numbers of impoverished, despairing people, both male and female — are seen as criminals rather than as sick.[16] It might be assumed that this response results because so many addicted poor people support their drug habits with crime, but the same behaviors in the middle-class community more often result in therapy rather than accusations.

The stark reality of this can be grasped by comparing the experiences of the poor, chemically afflicted pregnant women in the above report with those of a teenage boy from a white, middle-class family. Even though this is a story of one family, it is not atypical. After five years of behavior problems and drug use, a high school senior was admitted to a private drug treatment center in another town where he "recounted the wide range of drugs he had used, the lying, the cheating, the stealing, the vandalism, and even the drug peddling to support his expensive habit."[17] Despite these behaviors, this addicted teen in recovery and his parents were assured that they all were trapped in a cycle from which none of them could escape without help, since addiction was a disease over which the chemically impaired person had no control. At the same time, the parents learned that their son, probably born with a genetic predisposition to chemical addiction, had used drugs as a way to deal with the difficulties he experienced facing life in a sober state. His difficulties stemmed from his perfectionism and sensitivity.[18]

The juxtaposition of the two accounts is startling. One group is considered criminal because they turn to drugs to escape a life of poverty, a life that they despair of ever transcending. A middle-class teenager with the same addictions and criminal behaviors, precipitated by the inability to face life without chemical fixes, is considered sick. One group is prosecuted, convicted, and jailed. The other is nurtured, affirmed, and healed. Obviously there are situations between these two extremes, but such contrasts confront the realities of the classism and racism that lead to double standards in America's socioethical thinking about addiction.

Double standards also are founded on economic realities. Treatment for drug-impaired people in the middle class often is covered by their health insurance, and many have adequate personal funds. Widespread drug addiction among the middle class has engendered a whole new branch of the medical-industrial complex that fuels the economy.

In contrast, treatment for poor people, or for lower-income workers who have minimal to no insurance, is provided in nonprofit community programs that are funded by religious organizations, other charities, and tax-supported agencies. Of all the addicted persons who seek treatment, only one in eleven is admitted, and those denied care are disproportionately uninsured poor minorities in the inner cities.[19] For the poor racial and ethnic minorities who do gain entry to treatment programs, the therapy they receive and the therapists assigned to work with them may not fit their needs. According to Eva Bertram and Robin Crawford, drug treatment programs are designed and implemented by middle-class professionals who bring their own values and expectations to the therapeutic models they use. Thus both the design of therapy and the therapist-patient interaction may be inappropriate.[20] This certainly is not an intentional barrier to recovery, but it may cause difficulties for many addicted persons.

Other socioeconomic factors also affect levels of treatment in different communities. Many middle-class patients can take sick leave; working-class people lose income when they are not at work. Most salaried people can expect their jobs to wait for their recovery; most hourly workers cannot.

Thus, even though there is widespread addiction among upper- to middle-income urban, suburban, and rural people, larger numbers of chemically impaired persons in these communities can obtain adequate and appropriate therapy. Their access to care probably will increase, since considering them sick rather than criminal serves our economy and prejudices well.

In contrast, the urban and rural poor who are addicted do not have the resources — their own or the community's — to address their drug-induced afflictions. Increased access to care for this population would be expensive to tax-supported and nongovernment organizations. Considering them criminals rather than sick serves our prejudices well. Serving our prejudices does not in the long run serve the economy, however. The high costs of emergency room services for drug-related violence, the enormous drain on government funds to support the criminal justice system, and the loss of so many workers all add up to a hefty price tag.

National Abuse

Criminalizing the drug problem in neighborhoods populated largely by poor minorities also generates support for a "war on drugs." Bertram and Crawford point out that this war takes precedence over the civil liberties and human rights that America claims to model for the whole world. Since the onslaught of the war on drugs, not only suspected drug offenders but all criminal suspects in blighted urban areas are treated as less than citizens — indeed, sometimes as less than humans.[21]

Add to these troubling realities a claim that our government has promoted illegal drug supply to certain sociodemographic groups, and the "war on drugs" seems to be a misnomer for a war on the impoverished. According to one source: "There's a clear and unmistakable trail laced into the [Nicaraguan] contra connection [indicating] that drugs were indeed brought into this nation, into our ethnic communities, and . . . were sold to generate funds to fight covert wars."[22] Even without strong indications that this report is true, observations of the government's failed response to widespread addiction among the poor, especially among people of color, show why such accusations seem plausible. If Americans wanted to salvage the lives of whole communities where drug addiction is prevalent, we would realize that demand fuels supply. We would be opening treatment facilities instead of jails and addressing the conditions that make drug dealing seem for many like the only road to economic well-being.[23]

The drug trade contributes many riches to the national economy. As Americans we are enriched by the tobacco and alcohol industries, by their sales at home and increasingly by their sales abroad. These industries are legal and, like other industries, have the full support of our government. Bertram, however, reports that this nation's economy also is enriched by the illegal drug industries, an underground corporate world that has taken on all the structural complexity of legitimate corporations. Through money laundering and investments, as well as the incomes earned by the employees, this "surrogate economy" has generated revenues that filter into the whole economy.[24]

At the same time that America's tobacco and alcohol industries are protected and not impeded in their foreign marketing campaigns, the United States expends enormous sums and exerts strong political pressure to destroy the illegal drug industry that, by supplying Americans' drug needs, generates income for oppressed peoples who cannot make a living raising other crops.[25] The distinction between legal and illegal in this comparison has no *moral* weight. Addictive drugs are addictive drugs. Furthermore, evidence mounts that alcohol creates more havoc in the lives of more individuals and families, as well as in business and industry, than illegal drugs. And news reports almost daily indicate that tobacco creates health risks for all exposed. Here is another double standard that serves those in power and harms the oppressed, marginalized, and struggling ones among us.

If the so-called war on drugs were reducing the supply or use of illegal drugs, some might find the immoral tactics that are being employed acceptable. The fact is that we are expending huge sums and devoting much personnel to this effort, and all indications are that supplies and suppliers of illegal drugs have not been reduced one iota.[26] Meanwhile, the nation increasingly relies on income from this underground economy.

Thinking Ethically

The womenviews of human life found in part 1 provide mirrors with which to see this society's response to chemical addictions in a different light. They reveal that some among us find life so hopeless that their transcending creativity to overcome barriers to being fully human seems to be nonexistent. Dependence is seen as a problem rather than as the root reality of being human; and Christ is not recognized as the least among us who depends on our help. The lack of any long-term vision of justice and mercy for overcoming the painful socioeconomic conditions that promote drug use precludes a constructive divine-human cooperative effort. Failure to exercise power in interactive and enabling midwifery ways has resulted in strong-arm tactics that have been unjust and unmerciful and also fostered inappropriate treatment models.

Transcending Creativity

Of central importance for Christian ethical thinking about addiction is an ethic of life grounded in the transcending creativity that fosters well-being and crosses over barriers to being fully alive as human beings. Transcending creativity is God's gift to those created in God's image, and yet it is unknown intellectually and practically by large numbers of people who live in nihilistic circumstances that evoke only despair. Loss of the self-determining and self-surviving freedom inherent in transcending creativity, whether caused by external or internal factors, takes away the sense of power over life's circumstances.

Many persons without any sense of their own creating and transcending powers turn to drugs as an answer; addiction in turn robs them of the ability to exercise the very creating and transcending gifts they need. According to numerous studies, many persons become addicted for genetic or biochemical reasons; they too are robbed by drug impairment of the ability to use their creating and transcending gifts. Regardless of the reasons for addiction, to be freed of its impairing effects requires empowerment to find inherent in oneself the creative power to transcend that which robs one of being fully human, totally alive. The image of creating and transcending God is obscured in persons who are addicted, but like the sun on a cloudy day, it still exists. Response to persons who are addicted, then, should focus on enabling them to reclaim and enact that image of God. To do this, we must first be able to recognize God's creating and transcending image in ourselves and equally in the persons who are addicted.

Dependence

Womenviews of human dependence were founded on the idea that God depends on us and that Christ is found in the least among us, awaiting our response to human needs. This realization of where we find Christ not only sensitizes us to the plight of those who are oppressed, marginalized, and even brutalized by our system — a system that turns many to drugs for economic survival or personal solace. Seeing Christ in the least valued and most damaged among us also provides a norm by which to measure our society and a call for cooperative efforts to make life just and merciful for all. Without such understandings and actions, the problems of drug addiction will not be addressed.

Dependence understood as a moral category bestows different ways to think about human life and addiction. If dependence, instead of independence, were held up as normative of human life, some persons might not turn to drugs as a way to manage their isolated lives. They might know that it is acceptable to admit their need for help from others without being seen as weak. Indeed, the success of therapy groups such as Alcoholics Anonymous hinges on the affirmation that it is acceptable to *depend* on one another. This actuality needs to be named and affirmed not only in therapy but in the society at large.

Womenviews of dependence also bring critical discernment to the language used to describe addiction. In thinking, writing, and talking about addiction, the root problem often is defined as dependence. Anne Wilson Schaef says that "addicts tend to be dependent and to feel increasingly powerless and bad about themselves."[27] She continues by defining drug addictions as the intake of substances that are "almost always mood-altering and lead to increased physical dependence."[28] Schaef's thinking about dependence is concerned as much about the personality of the person who becomes addicted as about the psychological or physical needs of addicted persons for certain behaviors, objects, or substances. In either case, dependence is a problem of addiction for Schaef. An underlying assumption is that to be a healthy human is to be free from dependencies of any sort.

Clearly, the person who becomes addicted to a chemical substance is physiologically and psychologically dependent on it in the sense that the body and personality have been changed so that the person senses an ever-increasing need for the drug in order to survive. No doubt many chemically damaged persons also are socially dependent in unhealthy ways, in ways that deny their creating and transcending freedom and their power to be co-workers for justice and mercy. The difficulty arises when dependence is perceived to be the primary problem. From the perspective of womenviews, the primary problem with addictions is that they impair the abilities to be fully human as persons, fully capable as creative subjects of our divine-human destinies. Impairment, then, rather than dependence should be the greater concern.

Cooperation

Womenviews call for different models for responding to the drug crisis. An insight from womenviews that contrasts with the war-on-drugs response to widespread addiction is the understanding that our moral destiny always is to be God's co-workers toward a future we believe is just and merciful but never accomplished. In contrast, wars are intended to wipe out a particular problem at a particular time and place, like calling in the exterminator to get rid of the termite infestation that threatens our house. War is a short-range, single-agenda response to a problem.

The problems of drug-impaired persons and the marketing of drugs in all communities require a long-range, broad-agenda response. Drug addiction is as old as human history, and no doubt will continue to persist as long as fallible human beings exist. For those along the way who choose this route, compassionate and effective response always will be needed. To overcome the volume of drug use that is crippling so many today, however, we must "keep on keeping on" in every social structure of this society to prepare people to face life with self-assurance and self-supporting skills. Several generations surely will pass before drug addiction is no longer a scourge that threatens the whole fabric of the social order. As soon as Americans stop thinking in terms of war and start thinking in terms of cooperation for our divine-human destiny, we will turn the corner toward that long road to recovery.[29]

Power

The war on drugs also is called into question by the alternative ways of seeing power found in part 1. A war is waged with the intention to take control of the enemy and the enemy's possessions. Zero-sum mastery power is the operative philosophy. Combatants on both sides of the fray try to get the upper hand by disempowering the other. The drug war also includes the power of persuasion, which is used not only positively in educational programs to discourage drug use, but also negatively in government and media reports that cast poor minorities as the enemy. Yet everything that is known about the reasons for both the demand and the supply of drugs indicates that midwifery power is the primary need. Growers and peddlers need to be empowered to adopt legal ways of supporting themselves that provide a standard of living that is worth pursuing.[30] Addicted persons and persons at high risk of becoming addicted also need to be empowered for work that gives them a good self-image. Both disempowered groups need to be helped to find within themselves the power to face life and to embrace life with confidence.

Womenviews of power also mirror some aspects of many current treatment modes in a critical light. The requirement in most treatment groups and programs is that addicted persons release their addictions to a higher or external power. Addicted persons seeking help with the drug problems that have taken away their power to negotiate life are asked to turn away from the unhealthy power *over* them that the drugs have become and turn to another power *over* them that is believed to be healthier. In both cases, the operative understanding of power is that it involves mastery. Power is perceived as someone or something acting on someone or something. As indicated above, what addicted persons need is not alternate masters but midwives, to help them find the power *in* themselves to negotiate life without drugs.

Acting Morally

To address the drug crisis, life-affirming nurture must take place in every institution of society. The changed valuing and moral actions that affirm mothers and families, as advocated in the chapters on welfare and reproductive freedom, are needed to build self-esteem in women and children. Effective schools, job security, hope for a future for themselves and their families — all needed for women to have the freedom to choose birth — also are needed for all citizens to choose life rather than the escapism or marketing of drugs. In addition, children must be nurtured and educated in positive environments that nurture innate human abilities to be agents of life, justice, and mercy. Such preparation will enable more of the next generation to negotiate life's difficulties with their own resources so they will be less likely to seek addictive drugs as answers to life's challenges. Generations of cooperative efforts toward alternate ways of coping and positive methods of parenting and teaching will make a difference. This kind of response to the drug crisis is not a war but a birth.

9

HANDICAPPING CONDITIONS
Repercussions of Independence
and Productivity

Feeling the Pain

She moved as if every effort would be her last. Her coloring was ashen, her fingertips and lips were deep purple. The filth of the house revealed her inability to function, even though during my entire visit she kept getting up and trying to sweep some of the dirt from the floor. This left her breathless, unable to talk with me for several minutes after each effort. The children, in her care today while the grandmother who was raising them went shopping, were unattended.

I was making a home visit to talk with this young woman about having open-heart surgery to correct a valve damaged by rheumatic fever when she was a child. Her condition had reached crisis levels during her two pregnancies, but each time she had survived. Now, some three years after her youngest was born, she had canceled repeated appointments for admission at a research hospital, where state funds would pay for the surgical procedure to return her to health. I asked her why she kept delaying the surgery. "I'm going to die if they do the operation," she replied. I thought but did not say, "You're already dead. You cannot function as a normal human being. You're disabled and getting more so every day." She could not explain her premonition that she would die in surgery. I urged her to consider the needs of the children to have a mother who could care for them. I pushed her to deal with the pain her parents and children experienced as they watched her become more disabled day by day. I implied but did not state that she was being negligent as a mother — indeed, as a human being — by not taking the opportunity to make herself normal, to free herself from being so limited because of her heart defect.

My urging convinced her to have the surgery, scheduled for the following week. She died on the operating table. I cannot remember her name, but I will never forget the way I felt when I learned of her death. A mother myself, I thought of what her children were suffering. I grieved for her mother, whose only daughter was gone. But I rationalized my behavior toward her as being what was best for all concerned.

The same day, I visited a middle-aged woman who had given birth to her firstborn, a son with severe Down's syndrome. I was there to follow up an evaluation by the state child development program, to assure that the mother, Patricia, knew how to carry out the stimulation exercises and seek educational resources available in the area. Patricia told me her story. When John was born she had been urged by her physicians to let the baby die of benign neglect. When she refused this, she was told to institutionalize him, since he would never be anything but a vegetable. As a nurse whose training was at a state research and teaching hospital, where health professionals aimed to "fix" whatever was wrong, I sided with the doctors. I thought of the time and money and personal efforts the family as well as health and human resources would expend for this nonproductive human being who could not have a good life.

When John awoke from his nap, Patricia brought him into the room. He was severely retarded, nearly two years of age but behaving like a six month old. I asked Patricia to demonstrate her skills at some of the stimulation activities. As she and John interacted, I became enchanted with the love between them. Children with Down's syndrome, as I was to learn repeatedly by experience, often are abundantly loving human beings whose lavish outreach to all around them enriches anyone by whom they are touched. As I warmed to him, Patricia asked if I wanted to hold him. I was hooked in thirty seconds. The mothering side of me overtook the conditioning I had received as a nurse. I knew that as a mother, I would have made the same decision Patricia had made.

Patricia and John changed the way I looked at not only persons with handicapping conditions, but all people. My work in public health nursing increasingly involved persons living with limitations. Some were infants and children born with physical or mental challenges — Down's syndrome, cerebral palsy, spina bifida, rubella syndrome; others were children, young persons, and adults who had special needs because of disease or accidents — multiple sclerosis, blindness caused by diabetes, alcoholic neuropathy, paraplegia or quadriplegia due to automobile accidents; many were aging persons recovering from a stroke or a fracture. Even as I worked with individuals and families to enable persons with handicapping conditions to live as fully as possible with their situations, I no longer measured their value on the basis of how productive or independent they could be. Nor did I count personal and social costs.

Seeing the Realities

Persons with handicapping conditions constitute a sizable minority in the world and in this nation. In 1981, the UN's International Year of Disabled

Persons, 450 million people in the world had some kind of serious physical, mental, or emotional limitation. Estimates then were that by the year 2000, 600 million persons, a third of them children, will be living with disabilities.[1] In the same year, 47 million Americans were reported to be living with physical disabilities, and the federal Department of Health and Human Services had statistics showing that 60 to 70 percent "of the American population becomes either temporarily or permanently physically disabled at some point in their lives."[2] Recent statistics show that nationwide, 14 million Americans of working age have some kind of mental or physical needs[3] that require special adaptation on their or the community's part in order for them to exercise their abilities. In New Jersey alone more than 800,000 people (1 in 10) are living with such challenges, and "45% of New Jerseyans have potentially disabling conditions." Most adults living with special needs are unemployed, and those who are employed earn 14 percent less than persons without the same challenges. Because of their longer life span, more women (10.8 percent) than men (8.8 percent) are living with handicapping conditions.[4]

Despite their large numbers, persons living with permanent physical limitations are considered medical failures, social burdens, or oddities. Handicapping conditions are seen as so onerous that even some so-called pro-lifers who want to prohibit abortion except in cases of "problem pregnancies" believe that a deformed fetus, along with rape, incest, and threats to the mother's life, justifies abortion.[5] Laws have been necessary to protect the many babies born with severe mental or physical limitations from death by starvation or medical neglect.[6] Aging persons are denigrated because they no longer contribute to the gross domestic product. Children challenged by physical, mental, and emotional limitations have not been given adequate educational opportunities even though the law requires that these be provided. And capable adults whose special needs require adaptations and considerations in all areas of public life have had to work for legislation against physical and employment barriers so they can be full participants in our community at large.

Negative attitudes about persons with handicapping conditions are deeply ingrained in our cultural perceptions and our societal structures. Perceptions, shaped by fears or misinformation, in turn shape the way we interact with persons who have disabilities. Attitudinal and structural barriers, built to protect ourselves from those we fear and misunderstand, then prevent us from overcoming our negative perceptions.

Perceptual Barriers

Negative perceptions of persons living with handicapping conditions are reflected in many ways. Language is especially revealing. Despite many attempts by churches, interest groups, and legislative bodies to embrace persons with handicapping conditions, the way we speak and write reveals our actual sentiments. Because language can be hurtful and oppressive, I agonized over terminology as I began writing this chapter. One group that has paid attention to this matter considers terminology such as "handicapping conditions," used in this chapter, to signify the oppression of "handicapism."[7] (My reason for choosing this language in the title and in the chapter will become clear later in the chapter.) Another group decries the use of terms such as "persons with disabilities," since they claim the disabilities are socially constructed due to the fact that our world is designed so that persons living with special physical, mental, or emotional needs are excluded or marginalized.[8] Yet these same groups, which are composed of women, have labeled themselves "disabled women." Some try to use terminology such as "the specially-abled" to point out the extraordinary efforts involved in living a "normal" life with certain limitations. This has the danger of placing persons who have special needs on pedestals. Others speak of "the physically (or mentally) challenged," meaning persons who must use extraordinary efforts or methods to ambulate, manipulate, hear, see, speak, or understand.

The problem with all these terms is that they tend to *define persons* instead of *describe particular aspects of persons.* "Disabled women"; "the disabled"; "handicapped children"; "the handicapped"; "specially-abled person"; "the specially-abled"; "special-needs children"; "the physically challenged" — all these depersonalizing ways of speaking about persons with handicapping conditions are used in literature written by advocates. This illustrates how trapped we are in hurtful language.

Recent legislation offers insights into less hurtful language. The 1990 Americans with Disabilities Act (ADA), to be phased in by 1996, was crafted by government in league with persons having special needs and their advocates. The language is both definitive and descriptive. First, the person living with a handicapping condition is *defined* as an American — one of us, not an alien, not marginalized, but a citizen who is expected to participate in our common life. Second, the person is *described* as someone whose special needs caused by a disability are to be met by the larger community. The implications of both the language and the bill are that persons who have disabilities are invited and assisted — like all Americans (at least in theory) — to live as fully as their *abilities* will allow. This language is helpful, but continues to employ a negative term, *disabilities*, to describe persons living with particular challenges that most of us do not have. In this chapter I try to use language that emphasizes the personhood rather than the limitations of persons living with handicapping conditions.

Negative perceptions and definitions of persons with special needs are writ large in more than our language. The ways we relate to such persons speak volumes. Often people do not make eye contact with or directly address persons living with challenges; they act as if a person with special needs is a body without a personality, rather than an embodied and fully human being. Betty Medsger, herself a woman with a handicapping condition, reports that when adults living with challenges are addressed, sometimes they are spoken to as if they were children. Many who do not live with special needs seem to assume that persons with physical, mental, or emotional challenges cannot carry on a normal conversation. Medsger notes that some people who are willing to talk *with* rather than *at* or *to* persons having readily discernible challenges assume that the only topic should be the person's condition, rather than something the two have in common such as work, music, art, literature, the surroundings, or even the weather![9] Such behavior indicates our perception that having a handicapping condition means that one is not a *person.*

I watched a few years ago as a whole classroom of students in a seminary learned that physical challenges happen to *persons.* One student was severely affected by a neuromuscular disease. He sat in a wheelchair with difficulty. His limbs were spastic. His speech was slow, distorted, and usually not understood. Since the building was not accessible to his electric wheelchair, he was helped by a caretaker to negotiate steps to the main lobby where a manual wheelchair awaited. Thereafter, he had to be wheeled into class and out again, where he would wait for someone to come and take him to the next class, event, or home. If the next stop was on the second floor or lower level, one person carried his wheelchair while another helped him to negotiate steps. Due to the barriers in the building, this student was totally dependent physically. Due to his speech difficulties, he used a voice computer, so we all sat and waited for him to type in his comments in a class that was largely discussion. We were happy to wait, however, because his insights and wisdom were profound. Seminary residents were willing to accommodate the special needs of this student because they soon learned that he was a wonderful person. Before this experience many, if not most, of them probably would have avoided any contact with a person like this young man. Like most of us, they would not have looked at him, talked with him, or touched him; indeed, they would have ignored him.

Erroneous assumptions about the sexuality of persons with handicapping conditions also negate their full personhood, indeed, their very humanity. Persons having special challenges often are believed to be asexual.[10] A Canadian woman avows that women's groups say to her, "You're not a woman, you're a disabled person."[11] In the movie *Who's Life Is It, Anyway?* a young man, with a spinal cord injury that left him totally paralyzed from the neck down, was allowed to assume that he had no future sexual life, despite widespread research that has shown the sexual abilities of persons with his degree of neurological damage.[12] Unfortunately, this fiction fits the perception that most people have of persons with spinal cord injuries. A young woman with spina bifida, which causes neuromuscular damage in the lower body, asked her doctor whether she could enjoy sex. His response: "Don't worry honey, your vagina will be tight enough to satisfy any man."[13] Young men and women who are physically challenged to the point of needing to stay in the home with their parents are especially prone to having their sexuality denied.[14] In contrast, negative stereotypes and biases about persons with mental challenges sometimes have led to the mistaken belief that they are unable to control their sexual urges. Thus much effort has been expended by their caretakers — both professionals and families — to curb their social life and guard against any form of sexual expression.[15] To respond in such inappropriate ways to anyone's sexuality is to dehumanize all concerned. Humans are created to be sexual in the sense of relating to others through intimate body contact. If this aspect of life is denied persons, then part of their humanity is taken away.

Structural Barriers

Negative perceptions have led to several kinds of barriers that marginalize persons living with handicapping conditions. These excluding structures, societal and physical, affect persons with special needs at every age and stage of life.

Like the lepers of biblical times, children with special physical or mental needs often are "outside the camp" (Lev. 13:45–46).[16] Mainstreaming laws, requiring that all children ages three to eighteen with handicapping conditions have free and appropriate education in the most integrated possible setting, went into effect in 1976.[17] Yet many localities still have not instituted them fully. One school I worked with in public health in the early 1980s was exemplary, however. Most children with handicapping conditions spent part of their day in regular classrooms and part in a wing of the same school where the person in charge was a highly educated physical therapist who had cerebral palsy. She reminded all around her that *abilities* are what count. Often in such settings, children with cerebral palsy, spina bifida, muscular dystrophy, or visual or hearing impairment are segregated and assumed to be mentally retarded even though their challenges are entirely physical. With the advent of the Americans with Disabilities Act (ADA), America needs to educate all persons to their highest potential so that they can participate in and contribute to our common life.

Laws requiring mainstreaming in education, prohibiting physical barriers to public access, and mandating employment opportunities are designed to bring persons with special needs into the camp, inside the gate of America. Before these laws were instituted, persons with challenges requiring special needs were seen as so offensive that federal and state governments tended to institutionalize or support them in their or their parents' homes. This great expense to the public was preferable to having persons with handicapping conditions among us.[18] With this history, one cannot help but wonder whether strains on public funding mechanisms, more than advocacy groups, have been responsible for the changing laws related to persons with handicapping conditions, such as those set forth in the ADA of 1990.

The ADA is intended to remove physical and attitudinal barriers that impede the freedom of movement and exercise of abilities of all persons living with special needs that require of society appropriate adaptations. Included in the law are bans against discrimination in hiring, compensation, and advancement. The ADA also mandates that companies make modifications to enable persons living with special needs to participate fully in the job market.[19] This may seem like a large expense that companies are expected to bear, but two provisos in the law and several data suggest that the business community will not find the changes burdensome. The law specifies that the persons hired must be able to perform the jobs and that the adaptations required must not create undue hardships for the employers.[20] Data suggest that the costs to companies already hiring persons with handicapping conditions have been less than the benefits. The President's Committee on Employment of People with Disabilities reports that the average accommodation costs are less than five hundred dollars.[21]

Other information suggests that the business community may benefit from the new laws by exploiting job-seeking persons with handicapping conditions. A study of New Jersey companies, reported in 1992, showed that average annual earnings of all New Jersey men were $43,300; for men with special needs, $36,900. For all women in the state, average annual earnings were $26,200; for women with special needs, $22,900.[22] Even though the law protects workers with special needs from differential treatment related to salary and pay raises, employers see the new pool of workers as a way to find persons willing to work for minimum wage or in entry-level positions. Indeed, one employment research executive expressed delight that the ADA would provide "a new sector of the work force that we can take advantage of."[23] An employer believed that despite initial adaptation costs, "the return on investment is going to be there."[24] Past indicators suggest that, due to the difficulties of obtaining employment and a sense of responsibility to employers who made the adjustments to hire them, persons with special needs are less likely to change jobs.[25] Such realities can open the door to unfair wages and benefits.

Despite the potential for exploitation, many persons with handicapping conditions will benefit enormously from the ADA laws. Among persons having special needs, 23 percent are impoverished; this is triple the rate for the population as a whole. Many persons with special needs barely survive on food stamps, government checks, and public insurance. Nationwide, "3.2 million former workers who have become totally disabled receive an average of $7,125 a year from Social Security Disability Insurance." Three million other adults living with challenges, who have not worked enough to qualify for this insurance, exist on an average of $4,114 in Supplemental Security Income.[26] Since the early 1980s, denial and cancellation of benefits for persons living with challenges have been frequent, and many persons have had to go to court to have their only source of financial support and medical insurance instated or reinstated. Statistics and reports like these evidence that even with the lower salaries paid to most persons with special needs, for many their lives would be considerably enriched financially by employment. Public resources, such as Social Security, food stamps, and Medicaid, also would not be tapped as often if more Americans with special needs were employed.

Obviously, for most persons living with challenges the benefits of employment are more than economic. To be able to participate as full members of the society by contributing to the common wealth, developing their potentials, and supporting themselves is affirming of full personhood. Yet we should remain guarded about the ADA. Opportunities for injustice by private and public sectors are varied and numerous. Some persons with the special needs of handicapping conditions will have lower net incomes in the job market than on Social Security, due to extraordinary expenses of transportation and the tendency for exploitation by employers. With the present insurance laws in most states, many persons with special needs will not be insurable, so they will need to keep their government-sponsored health insurance despite employment income. Other special support services at home might be needed to enable a person to participate in the work force. Care must be taken that benefits to cover such expenses are not cut off just because a person is employed.

Also important to consider is whether a person's health is jeopardized by full-time or even part-time employment.[27] Some persons with special needs might be able to fulfill their potential as human beings better if they were not employed. In order to get off of public assistance, an artist might have to give up her low-paying but life-giving creative work that she scheduled around her special needs and take a job that demeaned or demoralized her. Persons living with handicapping conditions and their advocates need to think in terms beyond market-oriented economics and productivity.

Thinking Ethically

The unique moral challenges of persons with handicapping conditions give particular meanings to the norms discussed in part 1. Human freedom to be creators who transcend barriers to life takes on whole new meanings. The reality that life is necessarily more dependent for some of us must be accepted. Divine-human cooperation takes on wholly different connotations in certain situations. And power has extraordinary significance for persons with special needs.

Transcending Creativity

Persons with handicapping conditions are created in God's transcending and creating image. Even though they are living with physical, mental, or emotional challenges, they too are made by God to be creating and transcending artists of a world that fosters and nurtures life. Indeed, when we recognize the ingenuity required by persons with special needs simply to negotiate life, then we must subsequently recognize that such persons set standards of transcending creativity that few of us can match.

Our culture has erected so many barriers — emotional, social, educational, structural — to interfere with fully human life for persons living with challenges that extraordinary measures of creativity by all of us are needed to transcend them. Only thus can all the creating and transcending abilities of persons with handicapping conditions — abilities entrapped in the cages others have built — be freed, thereby enriching all of us, allowing all of us to be fully human beings. Our collective humanity is dependent on such transcending creativity.

Dependence

The views of God's and humanity's dependence that were explicated in part 1 reflect the reality that persons with handicapping conditions are *persons* whose needs require that they depend on others — for adaptations of our common space or for actual help in various activities of daily living. What is required is a full embrace of those persons who depend on us to make the adjustments and provide the special care for their needs to be met. The fact is, however, our love of independence probably makes this very difficult to accept. If God is seen as dependent, perhaps human dependence can be seen differently. Indeed, with a little imagination it would be possible to say that God has multiple handicapping conditions that require our response. Like the adult with quadriplegia or progressive multiple sclerosis, God has no hands to manipulate things or feet to navigate — except ours. Like the child with cerebral palsy, God cannot speak clearly — we must listen carefully to one another and our world to hear. Our faith teaches that God sees and hears all, but when prayers go unanswered or the world seems in total disarray, we wonder — Is God deaf and blind? Most assuredly, our faith knows that God is waiting and needing in and with the disempowered and hurting ones among us. God lives with special needs that only we can meet.

All of us are dependent at some times in our lives: infancy, very old age, during illnesses and injuries throughout our years. We seem ready to accept such temporary dependence. We are less willing to accept persons who are permanently dependent. Christian faith gives mixed messages in regard to persons living with permanently handicapping conditions. On the one hand, Christians are called to go outside the camp, as Jesus did when he sought and included persons whose handicapping conditions, according to the beliefs of that time, rendered them unfit to be among the community of the faithful. On the other hand, scripture says that Jesus did not leave persons with their handicapping conditions; he healed them. Before they were healed, Jesus loved them; but only after they were healed did they become part of the community that had excluded them. Handicapping conditions that are permanent, whether from birth, accident, or illness, cannot be healed. No amount of modern medicine or faith in God removes most handicapping conditions that require of us the meeting of special needs.

Therefore, those of us who do not live with special challenges are the persons who need to be healed so we can bring persons living with challenges inside the gates we have erected, gates that exclude them and complicate their lives. We need healing for our fear of dependence and our denigration of dependent persons. We need healing for our fear of persons who are different or who call upon us to be different. We need healing to become one with our sisters and bothers who have special needs due to conditions that are beyond their or anyone else's control. We even need healing to accept the fact that many things in life are beyond our control. Our needs for healing must be met in order for us to think and act ethically toward persons who are dependent due to permanently handicapping conditions.

Cooperation

Reflection on our divine-human destiny to be co-workers for justice and mercy reveals that other philosophical or psychological barriers also must be transcended. In order to think ethically and act morally regarding persons living with handicapping conditions, Christians need to come to grips with the way we in this culture measure human worth according to productivity. We have come to value persons on the basis of what they contribute to our *economy*, rather than what they contribute to our *humanity*. Thus productivity, rather than cooperative efforts for justice and mercy, has become the measure of human worth. Children are seen as potential producers of goods and services. Adults are expected to be producers of goods and services, and their worth is measured according to their economic gains from this activity. Elderly persons are tolerated because they have made their contributions of goods and services, more so if their wealth indicates a large measure of productivity during their working years.

This society needs goods and services; our existence depends upon the work that produces them. Yet, as seen in the chapter on welfare, we are selective in the work that is valued; and if no income is generated from human labor, it is not even considered work. For some persons with severely handicapping conditions, the very work of living is a full-time occupation. They are necessarily self-caretakers whose labors should be valued. In contrast, many persons with handicapping conditions can be as productive as any of us if they are provided education to nurture their abilities and if transportation and work-place modifications are made to meet their special needs. As more and more persons living with challenges enter the labor force, our valuing of them as productive citizens will grow.

These same productive folks are able to be co-workers for justice and mercy in ways that are readily recognized. For example, groups of persons with related special needs have banded together to support one another and challenge the physical and social barriers the rest of us have erected. But what of the persons living with conditions that are progressively worsening or that seem to preclude both employment and discernible co-operative efforts toward justice and mercy? How do they work with us for the common weal? How do they fulfill their share of our common moral destiny? The measure of each person's contribution toward our common life is God's alone, not ours. Perhaps the infant with Down's syndrome fulfills his moral obligation by showing us how to accept persons with mental challenges. Perhaps the young man with a severe neuromuscular disorder has the moral destiny of teaching us not to be afraid of our own dependencies. Perhaps the young woman challenged by life itself because of a defective heart valve teaches us something about life and death that we do not want to learn. Each has helped to shape the moral views of human life that are expounded in this book.

Power

Midwifery — the interactive cultivation of the powers that are inherent in all persons — is a pivotal moral norm for ethical thinking about persons with handicapping conditions. Without such power, many with special needs cannot live fully as transcending creators who are God's co-workers. In thinking ethically about persons with handicapping conditions, however, a very different kind of empowerment than the one permeating the previous chapter on addiction becomes operative. In the chapter on addiction, the concern was people who are impaired due to substance addiction. The goal was to "normalize" addicted persons — in other words, to empower them to be rid of their drug impairment so that they could live fully human lives. Although it was shown that their healing depended in large part on a change of our collective behavior, making personal and social adjustments to enable persons to live with drug impairment was not seen as a moral response. Even the language expresses the difference. The terms "addicted persons" or "drug-impaired persons" were seen as appropriate because addiction quite literally takes over and defines the person.

Thinking ethically about persons who are impaired due to handicapping conditions reveals that appropriate moral responses should empower persons so they can live fully human lives, maximize their abilities, and contribute their creativity and cooperation to our life together. But persons with special needs related to handicapping conditions cannot be "normalized." Instead, changes must occur in ourselves and in our collective lives to accommodate the special needs of persons with impairing limitations. Thus empowerment takes on very different connotations.

This chapter is entitled "Handicapping Conditions" for reasons that could not be explained until this point in the discussion. Persons living with special needs compel the moral response of a handicap. Since "handicapism" is used to define the oppression of persons challenged by their particular limitations, how can it be moral to give them a handicap? The thesaurus on my word processor provides some clues. The noun "handicap" is synonymous with disempowering words such as "affliction," "barrier," "disadvantage," "impairment," "impediment," and "limitation"; but also, with empowering words such as "advantage," "boost," and "edge." The verb "to handicap" has as synonyms both negative words like "disable" and "hinder" and positive words like "balance," "concede," and "equalize."

With these various synonyms of "handicap" in mind, we can turn to the game of golf to illustrate how both the empowering and disempowering, the positive and negative words can reveal a way to be midwives with persons who have special needs. In golf, each player has a handicap, which is a number designating the difference between that player's average score and an idealized (or even-par) round. A golfer's handicap, then, scores her or his limitations. When a round of golf is played, those persons with great skill (low handicappers) concede a numerical handicap or edge to those with less skill (high handicappers) so that all are on equal footing when the game begins. In the game of life, none of us is perfect; each of us has handicaps in the sense of limitations. Those of us with low handicaps have a moral responsibility to play in ways that empower those with high handicaps; in other words, we must cede to them an advantaging or boosting handicap that balances limitations so that all of us can exercise our abilities equally.

In the past, persons living with challenges have been understood to have a handicap in the sense of a disadvantage or impediment; such persons were defined only in terms of limitations. This is a distortion born of our unwillingness to embrace and empower all members of the human community. Womenviews lead to the realization that "handicapping conditions" compel the empowering actions of an equalizing handicap, not the disempowering actions of a limiting handicap as has been the case in the past. This way of thinking has turned the word "handicap" upside down to describe not the impairment of a person with special challenges, but a moral imperative that levels the playing field of life.

Acting Morally

Some of the empowering handicaps needed by persons living with special needs already have been accomplished in laws enacted over the past twenty years. But individuals, political organizations, and business establishments will try to find loopholes in the laws so that they do not have to provide the handicaps — the empowering advantages — needed by persons living with challenges. Thus advocacy on all levels must continue. Laws for adequate and inclusive education that were passed in the 1970s still have not been implemented fully, and when the economy is weak they will be further eroded or delayed because local, state, and federal leaders will not want to take action that will seem (albeit mistakenly) to limit the empowered in order to give an equalizing opportunity to those who have been disempowered. Barrier-free buildings and public facilities are not universal in this land because too many are not willing to allow the handicaps that balance our limitations. Employers will seek excuses not to hire or keep workers with special needs if their co-workers do not accept them due to their differences or if no economic advantage to the employer is realized. Thus, watchfulness and advocacy will be ongoing needs.

In order for society as a whole to accept the necessity to give an empowering handicap to persons living with challenges, more is needed than laws, definitions of legal requirements, and advocacy to assure that laws are obeyed. We the people need a change of heart and mind. Yet I do not know of a single local congregation of any denomination that has offered children or adults educational programs designed to help members overcome their fears, be healed of their barrier-creating ways of thinking and acting, and embrace all persons regardless of abilities, special needs, or appearances. I live in one of the most populated regions of the nation, but I have not read or heard of any public forums for such educational purposes, except those being conducted the last two years in business communities to prepare for meeting the requirements of the ADA laws.

Moral education is not just a head trip, however. As advocated in chapter 1 and modeled in each chapter in part 2, passion or emotion — pain, fear, anger, disgust, remorse — precedes new ways of thinking and acting. Educating ourselves to be givers of empowering handicaps to persons with special needs begins with face-to-face encounters with the very ones we have avoided.

Imagine the learning children would achieve if their teacher were in a wheelchair, their doctor wore braces and used crutches, their librarian were blind. Imagine the passion that would be engendered if the same children learned about the injustice and cruelty their teacher, doctor, or librarian has had to endure all her life because of handicapping conditions that in no way interfered with the abilities needed to attain her education and perform her job. Multiply this by every institution in which we visit, learn, work, worship, or play and we may be ready to embrace and empower persons with all levels of abilities and limitations.

10

CATASTROPHIC DISEASES
Rethinking Human Care

Feeling the Pain

I dreaded the twice weekly visits I made to Hannah's home to provide hospice-related nursing services. Her negative attitude was a barrier to effective care. I did not blame Hannah for her behavior. I wondered if I would act any better under the same circumstances. She was only five years older than I, and this made everything more difficult for both of us because her life was ending and mine was in high gear. Hannah had terminal cancer. It had started fifteen years earlier in one breast; then the other; then the cancer spread to other organs. By the time I began visiting her she was bedridden due to wasting, weakness, and metastasis to the central nervous system.

During the time that I knew Hannah, her situation was truly tragic. She had married a man fifteen years her senior. They had no children and were at great distances from family members, both geographically and socially. She had not cultivated a circle of neighbors and friends because her whole adult life had been devoted to a civil service job from which she had planned to retire after thirty years, so she and her husband could enjoy traveling when he retired. I had the sense that both she and her husband had been working all their lives in unpleasant jobs to earn the joy of retirement. Now she knew she would not be alive for that. She was understandably bitter.

She also struggled with role reversal. Even though she had always worked outside the home, she also had taken care of the home and her husband's needs. Through the years, she had assumed that she would care for her older husband when he became aged or ill. She could not accept her dependence on him for all of her care and support.

Unintentionally I evoked her bitterness on every score, sometimes for reasons that in retrospect probably were preventable if I had been more sensitive to Hannah's deep feelings of loss. Once she asked me how long I had been a public health nurse. I told her I had started ten years earlier, at age thirty-five, after my children were all in school. The fact that I had started a new life at the same age her cancer was diagnosed just rubbed salt into her wounds. One day I called to say I was going to be an hour late. When I arrived I explained that I had taken an hour of personal leave to get my driver's license renewed. She started weeping. I apologized for being late and upsetting her. Her private-duty, home-care aide took me aside and said her driver's license renewal form had come in the morning's mail, and she realized that she would never drive again. Another day she was very testy. I asked about it, and she said, "Do you go to church?" I proceeded to tell her about all the exciting and creative work I was doing in the church. She requested that I leave. Her aide went out the door with me. She said Hannah's minister had come to visit that morning and had told her that if she had enough faith she would be healed. He had added in parting that she must be hiding some terrible sins for God to be punishing her this way. The aide said this was not the first such visit with the same kind of message. I asked the aide to tell Hannah I would come back the next day to perform the nursing service. I hoped to be able to broach the religious question with her, but knew I could not push it. I was so angry at the minister that I wanted to call him up and give him a piece of my mind. As I drove back to the health center and reflected on the situation I could see Hannah's attitude problems in whole new ways.

Early the next morning I received a call from Hannah's husband saying she had been admitted to the hospital. I tried to go see her, but she was refusing all visitors. Hannah died three weeks later.

Hannah was not the only patient with terminal cancer whom I tended in public health. Indeed, I worked with home-based hospice patients almost daily in the early 1980s. Since much of my earlier nursing had been in pediatrics and emergency room, and I continued to serve children with leukemia, Hannah certainly was not the youngest patient I had seen dying. Neither was she the first terminally ill patient I knew whose minister or church associates had suggested that her loss of health was due to lack of faith or God's punishment. Over the last dozen years I have puzzled over why Hannah was so problematic for me. I have wondered if it was her honesty. She did not try to mask the pain and anger evoked by her catastrophic disease or the sense of loss that she experienced almost daily as the ability to live slipped away bit by bit.

In the 1970s and early 1980s, most of the dying patients I served had cancer. Today, cancer continues to be just as devastating a disease, and breast cancer reaches ever-higher tolls. But if I were in public health nursing now, the catastrophic diseases that would take most of my time and energy would be those related to AIDS (acquired immunodeficiency syndrome), which include many infections and cancers and cause the same robbing of life that is too young to die. Hannah's unfinished life, her anger, the externally imposed guilt, her choice of isolation, and her deep sense of lost opportunities are seen over and over among persons suffering with AIDS.

My experience with her, more than with any other person in the hospice program, has enabled me to see the AIDS crisis in human dimensions.

Seeing the Realities

AIDS[1] is the paradigmatic catastrophic disease of our time; it also is our paradigmatic moral failing. One person has astutely observed that there are two AIDS epidemics, "one created by stigma, and the other created by a virus."[2] These two interrelated facets of the AIDS crisis have within them many dimensions. Here the focus is on the human, female, contextual, and moralistic dimensions of AIDS that together call us as a nation to a more healing approach.

Human Dimensions

AIDS is a disease of human beings — not of certain groups. At first, AIDS was believed to be a "gay disease" because in the United States and Europe the earliest diagnosed cases were in sexually active gay men. Then AIDS was recognized as a disease of injection drug users. (The term "injection" refers to intramuscular, subcutaneous, and intravenous modes of administration.) Next came the rude awakening to the extent of the disease in children, women, and men due to blood transfusions or blood derivatives received before the human immunodeficiency virus (HIV), which causes AIDS, was identified and detected in the blood supplies. And there were the babies with HIV/AIDS, born of women who had been infected by injection drug use, male partners, or blood transfusions.

HIV/AIDS is a disease found in every aspect of the population and is transmitted by the exchange of body fluids such as blood, semen, and breast milk. The disease can be spread by the sex act from men to women, men to men, women to men, women to women; by needle sharing among drug users; by women to their babies in pregnancy, birth, or lactation; by the infusion of blood and blood products to anyone. Worldwide statistical estimates are that HIV infection in *adults* is transmitted by heterosexual sex (71 percent), homosexual sex (15 percent), injection drug use (7 percent), blood products (5 percent), other means (2 percent).[3]

HIV can live in the human body for years before any signs of AIDS occur. Thus it can be spread unknowingly. One of the stories heard repeatedly from persons infected with HIV is that they had injected drugs when they were in high school or college, had gone through withdrawal and treatment, and were on their way to a new life. Then their long-dormant HIV was discovered as they began to develop the cancers and other diseases that signal AIDS.[4]

When I worked in student health in 1982, I asked the doctor if we should be watching out for AIDS among the sexually active college students, including an average percentage of gays and some drug users. He said no, since the medical establishment believed at that time that the virus was found only in Haitian men who were gay. Seven years later, shortly before the end of the semester at another university, I attended a rally for AIDS awareness; widespread infection with HIV among college students nation-wide was cited. Due to the long incubation period of HIV, we as a nation have yet to reap the repercussions of the refusal to recognize that AIDS is a human disease that affects people in every socioeconomic, ethnic, racial, and sexually preferenced group.

In Africa and Asia, sexual transmission from the beginning of the AIDS epidemic has been almost entirely through heterosexual intercourse. Since one study has demonstrated that men are nearly twice as likely to infect women as the reverse,[5] the disease probably is spread largely by men to their multiple female partners. In these cultures (as in almost every culture worldwide), even if women are educated about the fact that proper con-dom use offers the best protection, and even if they are fortunate enough to be able to obtain condoms, they have little leverage to demand that their male partners adhere to safer sex practices. Breast feeding by HIV positive women sometimes infects those infants who were not already in-fected at birth. Many third-world nations do not have the financial and health care resources to test for HIV, diagnose AIDS, teach prevention, practice healthy hospital and clinic techniques, and screen the blood sup-ply. Thus in these impoverished nations HIV/AIDS runs rampant, along with equally devastating diseases such as malaria, cholera, malnutrition, and starvation, the extent of which makes exposure to HIV almost guar-anteed to result in rapid demise with the multiple catastrophic diseases that are called AIDS.[6]

Female Dimensions

AIDS is a women's disease. In the first six months of 1992, one million new cases of AIDS in adults were reported in the world, and half of these were in women. Estimates are that by 2000, around the world more women than men will have HIV.[7] According to the New Jersey Women and AIDS Net-work, in the United States 73 percent of the recognized and reported cases of women with HIV are in women of color, and many of these are poor. Under-reporting of cases in white, middle-class women is suspected, due to both the stigma of the disease and the failure of the medical establish-ment to identify HIV early in women. In New Jersey, AIDS is the most frequent cause of death among African-American women in their child-bearing years; New Jersey also "has the greatest incidence of HIV infection among women" in the United States. In the New York metropolitan area, "AIDS is the leading cause of death among women."[8]

Statistics such as the ones cited above show that women are now at the highest risk; yet in the United States, HIV infection in men and infants has been the primary concern. Indeed, women have been either ignored or seen only as vectors of the disease, as responsible for AIDS in heterosexual men and in infants. Thus one observer has written:

> Women with AIDS or HIV infection have been judged as bad mothers and wives, or simply as bad women, because they are viewed in the media and in the minds of many Americans as the vectors by which HIV is transmitted to men or children. Rather than looking at HIV infection as a threat to a woman's own future health, it is explained in terms of the other people in her life who she is thought to have put in danger.[9]

A typical way of thinking about women and HIV/AIDS was exemplified by a church I attended. The members were establishing a hospice for men living with the last stages of AIDS and had decided that their next project would be a home for infants and children infected with the disease. No one seemed to ask whether the mothers of the babies needed care or other women without babies might be living and suffering with the disease.

Because women with HIV infection have recurrent disease patterns that in 1992 still were not classified as AIDS, one slogan heard among people who serve women with HIV is: "Women don't have AIDS, they just die from it." This problem has occurred in part because AIDS was first identified in the United States among gay men, and their symptoms became the standard for the official Centers for Disease Control (CDC) diagnosis of the disease. Obviously, men cannot have recurrent and incurable infections and cancers of the female genitalia and pelvic reproductive organs. Women can; and women with HIV usually do. Women also are subject to the same disease complexes that *are* classified by the CDC as AIDS — particular opportunistic infections, cancers, and conditions seldom seen in people whose immune systems have not been compromised by HIV.[10]

The CDC's refusal to recognize that HIV/AIDS disease patterns are gender-specific has had both medical and social ramifications. Doctors who are not aware of female patterns of the disease do not test for HIV when treating women with recurrent yeast infections or pelvic inflammatory disease. This delays both diagnosis and appropriate treatment. Meanwhile, the women are unaware of their positive HIV status and may spread the disease unintentionally. Because HIV/AIDS was ignored in women, for the first ten years of the epidemic, clinical studies largely excluded women; and the first drug trials to include women were on pregnant women — the concern was finding ways to prevent the spread of HIV infection from women to their babies during pregnancy and at birth, with the health of women being only a secondary consideration.

Defining AIDS primarily in relation to males also has had societal ramifications. Many women have been and continue to be unable to qualify for AIDS-designated economic support and medical services. For years, HIV-infected women died from incurable infections and rampant cancers without ever having received these services. In 1992 the Social Security Administration changed its eligibility rules for AIDS support, diverging from the CDC definition so as to cover more persons with HIV who were too ill to work. In addition, failure to count the specific female symptoms of women with HIV as AIDS has falsified the actual number of cases of the disease and helped to continue the mistaken belief that AIDS is a gay men's disease. Indeed, because the U.S. disease classification has been based solely on the symptoms that were identified in gay men, statistics still show that 58 percent of AIDS cases in the United States are due to male homosexual sex.[11]

Although women are twice as likely to be infected by men as the reverse, not all women have HIV/AIDS solely because of their male partners' use of injected drugs or numerous sexual encounters. Nevertheless, women's roles as vectors have been overemphasized. For example, prostitutes were blamed for spreading the disease in the heterosexual population. Yet Ines Rieder and Patricia Ruppelt cite studies that show that after a year of educational efforts, European and American prostitutes who were not drug-impaired had an infection rate of less than 1 percent. In Africa and Asia, prostitutes also have responded well to educational campaigns about safer sex.[12] Lynn Hampton reports that, on the one hand, most prostitutes who are not drug-addicted protect themselves and charge enough to refuse customers who will not practice safer sex. On the other hand, she has found that women who "turn tricks" to support their drug habits are so desperate for a fix that they cannot afford to deny customers who refuse to practice safer sex; and they generally are less able to control the sexual act. If their drug habits include needle-sharing, the women also may be infected by that route.[13]

While studies have demonstrated that nonaddicted prostitutes know how to protect themselves, unsuspecting women who are in sexual relationships with men whom they assume are faithful are at far greater risk of infection. Many men have multiple sex partners, and few are honest with their wives or lovers about other sexual encounters or drug habits.[14] Even when women do suspect or know of risky behavior on the part of their partners, however, few have enough power in the relationship to insist that men practice safer sex with them; nor do they dare question what other sexual activities or what drug habits their partners have.[15] Some women in every American subculture are radically disempowered in their sexual relationships. Imagine a battered woman — and they come in every socioeconomic stripe — trying to control the kind of sexual activity she and her male partner have. Many battered women are routinely raped by their partners.

Regardless of the means of transmission, when women of childbearing age have HIV their babies are at risk of being born with the infection. Statistics provided by the New Jersey Women and AIDS Network indicate that the risk factors of prenatal/perinatal mother-to-infant infection range from 7 to 40 percent, with an average of 30 percent. In Newark, New Jersey, the average risk of mother-to-infant infection is 18 to 22 percent; in Europe it is 14 percent.[16] Many people assume that if a woman knows she has HIV, she will not get pregnant, or, if she learns of her infection after she is pregnant, she will want an abortion. Such assumptions include the belief that all women submit to HIV testing, that all women have access to prenatal care, that all women have the autonomy to make such decisions, and that all women hold to white, middle-class values.

The fact is, many women learn of their own infections after their babies have become sick and been diagnosed with HIV/AIDS. Many more women have cultural settings — and this includes U.S. women — where their only reason for being is to bear and rear children.[17] If such women learn that they are HIV positive, they might just as well contemplate suicide as abortion. They pray for their baby to be one of the 70 percent or more who escape the disease so that they can fulfill their maternal purpose. Women who live in severe poverty that threatens their very survival, both in the United States and around the world, may choose to have a baby even knowing about the disease, even after losing a baby to it and suffering the ill effects of the disease themselves, because they hope to have a disease-free child who will survive them.[18] This is an ancient form of human immortality that is not superseded by religious beliefs. Like all God's creatures, we have a deep sense that our survival depends on our progeny.

Despite the fact that women who are HIV positive are not required by law or medicine to receive an abortion, many feel coerced to make that decision. For some, it seems like a form of genocide for their race.[19] Women who make the decision to continue their pregnancy after learning they are HIV positive, or who decide to get pregnant despite their infection, make their risky choices — for themselves and their babies — with the longing that a cure will be found before it is too late for both of them.

Contextual Dimensions

Many breakthroughs do engender hope. Drugs are being developed to extend the life span of persons living with HIV infections, to improve their immune systems and slow or cure the opportunistic infections and cancers that take advantage of deficient immune systems.[20] Some therapeutic regimes also show promise of reducing the transfer of the disease from mother to baby. Sexual transmission is greatly reduced by the use of latex barrier methods and safer sexual practices. Some enlightened school systems provide condoms. In a few nations where the sex trade is prominent, prostitutes are being taught to use condoms, and their health is being monitored. A few wise nations and some U.S. communities provide clean needles to drug addicts; many more teach drug users how to keep their drug-administration equipment infection-free.[21] In nations with adequate health resources the blood supply is tested for the virus; this has almost eliminated the danger of spreading the disease through transfusions or other blood products.

These glimmers of hope that bode well for the future must not mask the present reality that AIDS is a biological disease that has catastrophic social and economic consequences on those who live and die with it, their families, their friends, their communities, and the whole society. The AIDS epidemic has become a crisis of unmanageable proportions because we were not willing to face reality, and then we found ourselves ill-equipped to deal with reality when it hit us in the face. As I reflect on the AIDS crisis, I realize that it is intimately related to all the other social crises discussed in this book, crises that when seen through the lenses provided by the AIDS epidemic take on new dimensions. As Naomi Schapiro pointedly remarks: "AIDS only puts the sickness of our society into sharper focus."[22]

The welfare system encourages men with low-paying jobs to leave women and children they cannot afford to support. With few exceptions, instead of supporting two-parent families, America offers minimal existence and health care benefits to women and children only after male providers have left. As discussed earlier, the level of AFDC benefits paid to women with children is so low that some women have ever-changing partners as a means to survive. This places them and their partners at higher risk for HIV/AIDS. At the same time, men who have left their wives or live-in partners are likely to have an increased number of sexual liaisons, also adding to the likelihood of more HIV infections. Statistics show widespread infections of HIV/AIDS in impoverished populations in and around New York, Newark, and other cities where a majority of welfare recipients are ghettoized minority women and children.[23] Thus racism, classism, and an abortive system of support for families in trouble can be blamed for some of the spread of HIV/AIDS.

Also seen in the chapter on welfare was the fact that care-giving is denigrated, so there are insufficient persons to care for those who are ill in their homes. Family leaves usually are not possible either. Many with AIDS have no source of care except in public institutions.

Timidity about teaching sex education in the schools and assuring that all young people have access to affordable birth control has built a barrier against making condoms available to prevent the spread of HIV/ AIDS in our youth. In heavily infected areas, school boards have initiated programs of sex education, including the distribution of condoms and counseling on ways to decrease the risk of HIV infection. These actions have provoked outrage from churches and parents who believe that moral instruction and "Just say no!" slogans are sufficient deterrents to experimental or promiscuous youthful sexual encounters.

Because of a disjointed system of health care delivery, when the epidemic began, the United States was without a readily available network to organize a concerted response, to establish a sufficient number of anonymous testing and counseling sites, and to orchestrate the multifarious efforts. Furthermore, our patchwork health care system that mixes government and business forms of delivery leaves millions without adequate health care coverage that, if available, would provide the means to be informed, tested, observed, guided, and treated earlier and more effectively.

Failure to provide adequate therapy and enough treatment centers for almost 90 percent of drug addicts who seek help has allowed HIV/AIDS to spread faster in that population than might have been the case if treatment had been available. This nation also has resisted needle-exchange programs to prevent the spread of HIV/AIDS, because many have been concerned that such action would seem to sanction injection drug use or even encourage it. Some communities have offered such programs over protest; wider acceptance has been afforded efforts to teach injected drug users to keep their "works" clean.

The tendency to segregate certain groups or populations, in the same way that we have isolated and oppressed persons living with handicapping conditions, has led to stigmatization of persons living with AIDS in cruel ways that deny their humanity (and ours). This stigma comes in part from the fact that AIDS often is transmitted sexually, and despite the so-called sexual revolution, we still are made uncomfortable, even frightened by the reality of our sexuality in all its diversity. All life-threatening diseases carry a certain amount of stigma, because we fear death. Elisabeth Kübler-Ross reported in her writing and seminars of the 1970s that persons in the last stages of cancer were "untouchables" — neither family members nor health personnel touched them unless absolutely necessary. Persons in the last stages of AIDS often are young, and this makes their deaths even harder to accept. When death and sex come in the same package, as happens with HIV/AIDS, fears reach proportions that cannot be addressed except with the utmost care and patience on everyone's part.

Because of phobias about death and sex and multiple misunderstandings about HIV/AIDS, this disease has been handled differently than other infectious diseases in the nation's history. Some states offer anonymous testing for HIV infection. Persons who are concerned that they might be at risk of infection can go to a test center, have their blood drawn without providing any identifying information, and then return at a designated time to get the results and counseling. No contact identification is required if the test is positive, although many infected persons do notify their sexual or needle partners.

This may not seem to be a very effective way to stem the tide of such a catastrophic disease, but due to the way this society has responded to persons with HIV/AIDS, it is believed to be the only way to encourage people to be tested and counseled, and to change their behavior. Confidential, rather than anonymous, testing is being required of some populations; and there is constant legislative action to increase the use of confidential testing. But those who oppose required or confidential testing say that it will scare people away from health services and further spread HIV/AIDS. For instance, some women who believe they are at risk of HIV infection do not go for prenatal care at public health facilities. They fear they will be tested against their will and without their knowledge, and if found HIV positive, have their children placed in foster care, lose their public housing, or be ostracized by their communities of support.[24]

Moralistic Dimensions

Large-scale societal response to HIV/AIDS has been to blame the sick persons. In other words, persons with HIV/AIDS have been seen as deserving of the disease because it came about due to some action on their part. A somewhat more gracious space has been allowed for persons infected by blood transfusions, women infected by philandering or drug-injecting husbands, infants, the few people known to have been infected by one health care worker, and the less than one hundred health care workers infected by their patients. Yet these persons with HIV/AIDS also are stigmatized by their disease. One woman, who received the virus through a blood transfusion, recounts that her husband was fired when his employer learned about the infection, and she was isolated from her friends and her church.[25]

Fortunately, only rarely is personal moral culpability a question when people have other diseases that commonly kill many among us and deplete our economic resources. Even though smoking, improper diet, and lack of sufficient exercise are known to cause life-threatening heart conditions (America's number one killer) and some cancers, we do not think in terms of "innocent" or "deserving" people when it comes to these more socially accepted diseases. Because we have failed to accept the reality that HIV/AIDS is a disease of human beings rather than a just desert of particular groups or for certain behaviors, we have made HIV/AIDS a socially unacceptable disease.

The fact is that the persons first infected with HIV/AIDS were not aware of their risk of the disease at the time they engaged in the behavior or made the choices by which they were infected. Furthermore, as soon as the gay community, where HIV/AIDS was first diagnosed, learned of the mode of transmission, they engaged in a massive campaign to change behavior to protect against further spread of the disease. As stated earlier, Rieder and Ruppelt reported that prostitutes also responded rapidly and appropriately.[26] And despite the impairing impact of addiction, persons who inject drugs have responded favorably to the few efforts to help prevent the spread of HIV/AIDS among drug addicts. Lisa Berlin cites a 33 percent reduction in the HIV infection rate due to a needle-exchange program in New Haven.[27] In contrast, despite what we know about the relationship between deadly diseases and smoking, poor diet, and lack of exercise, not all Americans — even those who are informed about the risks — have changed their life-styles to healthy levels. Some people who have had multiple bypass surgery continue to eat improperly, fail to get adequate exercise, and even smoke. People with heart disease and cancer usually are not considered morally culpable; people with HIV/AIDS usually are. Here is a malicious double standard that ethical reflection shows to be unreasonable. All persons with life-threatening diseases deserve to be treated as human beings who are suffering and in need of our help.

Thinking Ethically

Each social crisis that has been considered in part 2 has given a particular meaning or emphasis to the moral guidelines of part 1. At the same time, the moral norms of part 1 have provided mirrors with which to see the social issues addressed in part 2 differently. The AIDS crisis also imparts its particular meaning to the norms of part 1: life-engendering and transcending creativity, dependence, divine-human cooperation for justice and mercy, and empowerment as the primary human reflection of God's power in our midst. These norms in turn reflect the AIDS crisis in new perspectives.

Transcending Creativity

Since many lives are so seriously endangered by HIV/AIDS, an ethic of transcending creativity devoted to the nurture and care of life is paramount in thinking about this social crisis. Estimates are that fifty to sixty thousand Americans are being infected with HIV each year, and soon that many Americans will be dying of AIDS annually.[28] Projections are that at least another decade will pass before we can hope for a vaccine or cure.[29]

To uphold an ethic of life as understood in this book means, first of all, that we are committed as a people to garner our creating and transcending abilities to prevent HIV/AIDS and, for those who already have the disease, to seek cures. Until these are accomplished, an ethic of life-fostering and transcending creativity compels us to alleviate suffering and give better quality to lives shortened by incurable disease. This way of thinking now guides the multifarious responses mounted by the medical-industrial complex and numerous other organizations, although that response still is inadequate. Until HIV/AIDS is prevented or cured, it is a disease that brings relentless human demise and death at an early age, and this requires appropriate personal and societal response.

Paradoxically, persons living with HIV/AIDS have provided some answers. Many of the accounts written by women with HIV/AIDS tell of being truly alive for the first time after they came to grips with the original devastation of learning they were infected with HIV. Realizing that their lives were short, they learned to live each day to the fullest. This did not remove their fear of disease and death, but the new lease they had on life was a gift.[30] Other women's stories were full of anger and grief, hopelessness and despair. Like Hannah who was dying with cancer, they were dying with HIV/AIDS. Knowledge of the disease, or the beginning of symptoms, was tantamount to a death sentence preceded by cruel and unusual punishment.[31]

As I reflect on these diverse responses to HIV/AIDS by the persons who are infected, I see two patterns that have profound moral implications. First, persons who were able to *live* more fully when they knew of their pending early death were those who had sufficient economic and social resources to creatively transcend some of their difficulties. Whereas those whose *deaths* began with knowledge of the disease grappled with socioeconomic circumstances that made HIV/AIDS just one more, albeit ultimate, barrier to life. A second factor, however, creatively transcended the first. Women who faced HIV/AIDS in loving and supporting communities, which demonstrated by their care of one another that they would be there when needed, found that they could *live* with the diagnosis despite numerous other hardships.

Recently I talked at some length with a Latina woman in her late thirties, a former drug user who had supported her habit by prostitution and had learned of her positive HIV status in jail. After a lifetime of economic struggle and a decade of drug addiction, she began receiving concerned care from many people due to her diagnosis. She expressed regret at her past behavior and sadness that she was beginning to get the infections that forecast death. Yet even though she was still struggling economically, being surrounded by people who cared for her as a valued person for the first time in her life caused her to embrace life with such gusto that her joy was contagious. People with HIV/AIDS can be helped to live until they die if they are surrounded by an empowering and supporting community.

Dependence

For some persons, the fear of being dependent as the diseases of AIDS progress may seem like an even greater problem than their pending death. Indeed, for some persons with HIV/AIDS, death promises personal release, whereas dependence is associated with loss of personhood. Our worship of independence — from government, from families, from peers, even from intimate loved ones — creates havoc in the midst of the HIV/AIDS epidemic. How do we help people accept their economic and physical dependence caused by the disease, so that they do not feel as if their very selves have been lost long before they die? How do we empower people to embrace dependence as the root reality of being human, not as loss of humanity? Clearly, communities of support on whom persons with HIV/AIDS can depend are central to overcoming the fear that loss of independence is loss of personal identity. Yet we need to enable people to *think and feel* differently about what it means to be human, a creature, so that dependence is not feared as death of personhood but accepted as an alternative way of life.

Cooperation

As already indicated, nowhere do we need more acutely the empowering work of cooperation — of God's power given in our work with and for our neighbors — than in our response to HIV/AIDS. For those who have eyes to see, many persons with HIV/AIDS represent the suffering, needing, and waiting Christ in the "least" among us, and our response to Christ is compelling. Yet a paternalistic or maternalistic nurturing of the sick by the well is not the answer. It is just such responses that make people fear dependence. Instead, what is needed is co-working, co-empowering interaction like that of Christ in and with the neighbor.

HIV/AIDS calls for a new way of seeing our moral destiny of being co-workers with God. This catastrophic disease requires us to work together in many ways for justice and mercy. Justice means equitable and fair treatment by every institution. Loss of employment, health insurance, and housing often follows the HIV/AIDS diagnosis, especially when symptoms become obvious. Safety nets are like welfare — minimal to totally insufficient — and often accompanied by the same stigma and harassment. Justice requires a different response to HIV/AIDS.

Mercy obviously has been absent in much of the HIV/AIDS epidemic. Yet mercy takes surprising turns. A physician recalled her residency at a New York hospital during the early years of the epidemic. She interpreted mercy to mean trying to find cures. Patients in great pain and already markedly wasted by AIDS were put through strenuous diagnostic procedures and subjected to sickening therapies in her determination to conquer a disease that was killing so many people her own age. One patient whose suffering was so immense that he kept begging her for help was scheduled for the maximum of procedures. After she left for the day a senior physician checked on the patient, canceled all the tests and treatments, and prescribed pain medication. The man spent his short remaining life in comfort and died in peace. It was a lesson in mercy that she never forgot.[32]

Power

The specter of HIV/AIDS urges us to muster all our powers to overcome human illnesses, and this we must continue. But such mastery ways of exercising power must be held in tension with the tenderness of life-enabling power that is like midwifery, the empowering interaction that is just as important in the transition of death as in birth — both of which are integral to human life.

Many care-givers who work with persons in the late stages of HIV/AIDS report the empowerment they receive from the ones for whom they are caring.[33] They have learned that power is not unilateral, but happens in the midst of merciful interaction. What is needed is co-empowerment among persons with HIV/AIDS and their advocates, caretakers, families, and friends.

How can we bring to birth the power that is in us all to meet the crisis of HIV/AIDS? Many groups and organizations are seeking ways to do this, but the supply is much less than the demand. How do we empower persons with HIV/AIDS to have a sense that they can fulfill their moral destinies, carry out their purposes for being? There are no simple answers to such questions, but the moral task is to ask the questions and together, with persons who have HIV/AIDS, to seek answers that will enable each person among us to *live* until she dies, at whatever age, due to whatever cause. HIV/AIDS is not a blessing anymore than it is a curse. If we approach it with faith and ask how to respond morally, however, we may find among ourselves the powers of life-fostering and death-transcending creativity and the cooperative efforts that are needed.

Acting Morally

How do we respond to AIDS when there is no ready cure, when we face such vast numbers of children and young adults who will be dying for at least the next decade? Our moral challenge is to act in response to clearly understood realities that counteract irrational fears, in relation to faithful ethical reason evoked by deeply felt passion. The specific actions that are called for by the catastrophic diseases of HIV/AIDS already are anticipated above. The crisis is so massive that we cannot begin to address here all that needs to be done, but some actions that seem especially important in the context of the priorities in this book can be highlighted.

If we as a people begin to work toward solutions to the social crises discussed in the chapters on welfare, reproductive choices, addiction, and handicapping conditions, then we will have some of the broader networks in place to prevent further spread of HIV/AIDS and to care for those who already are infected. If care-giving roles — in relation to children, aging parents, ill spouses, or dying friends — were valued and also garnered adequate income, more persons with HIV/AIDS would be able to remain in their or their families' or friends' homes. This care would have to be supplemented and supported by social programs, but an extensive network of persons is needed due to the degree of illness and numbers of dying persons. If broadly defined family leaves were legally protected, this would further the support network. Imagine a world in which an employee could go to her superior, request leave to take care of her lover who was in the final stages of HIV/AIDS, and not feel that her job or status in the company were threatened. If contraceptive and HIV information and protective supplies were readily available and affordable for all sexually active persons, the continued transmission of the disease could be slowed. The WIC (women, infant, and children) food program, where vouchers for particular foods are given when mothers attend their own or their children's clinic appointments, might serve as a model for this. Vouchers for condoms and other safer sex barriers, as well as contraceptives, would be dispensed in connection with affordable health services, education, and counseling about how to prevent sexually transmitted diseases as well as pregnancy. If drug treatment programs and appropriate therapies were widely available, and these centers of therapy also were points of refuge and places where needle exchange could take place, there would be a reduction in addiction as well as in the spread of HIV/AIDS among injection drug users. If the laws of the Americans with Disabilities Act — which do cover persons living with HIV/AIDS — were accepted and fully implemented, then, as the disease gradually produced handicapping conditions, persons with AIDS would be able to remain in employment longer. With new drug regimes that extend life span, the likelihood that persons with HIV/AIDS can continue employment is increasing.

Human care, then, is not simply the way we tend the needs of particular persons who are ill with life-denying diseases. Human care requires the structuring of a network of institutions that are merciful and just and provide a safety net that is truly supportive of human life in its broadest dimensions. Then when a disease such as HIV/AIDS comes along, we are prepared to care for all those affected so that a catastrophic disease does not become a societal catastrophe.

Epilogue

Probably the most challenging painting I ever did was commissioned by a physician who lived nearby. She wanted a large picture of magnolias to go on a particular wall in her newly redecorated living room. I was invited to her house to see the lighting and the colors in the room. A muted beige predominated with touches of color: cadmium orange; yellow ochre; cerulean blue; and abundant greens of lush houseplants and evergreens beyond the glass walls. The time was late summer, and the place was southern Virginia, where huge evergreen magnolias bloom until frost. I proceeded to drive about town seeking flowering branches from magnolia trees. I made new friends as I knocked on doors and begged a piece of the greenery in their yards.

I limited the pigments of my palette to the shades of orange, yellow, blue, and green that I had seen in the room. By choosing a palette of colors designed for a particular setting, I found my creative powers at their best. I mixed the warm and cool colors to create soft shadows in the flowers. Contrasting pigments were combined to make rich hues and deep contours in the leaves. With an impressionistic flare I mottled the orange, yellow, blue, and green in pale tones to catch the sunlight that filters through the leaves.

I presented the finished painting to the owner with joy. She was shocked. She had pictured the magnolias on a black background, like a tray she used in the dining room. I offered to cancel the contract, but as she stood there debating with me about it, she became ever more captivated by the painting. She decided to try it out for awhile. Soon the check arrived in the mail. She too had felt the joy I experienced with the painting, which may have been the most creative work I had done to that time, precisely because I limited the pigments. The self-limited palette became a technique that was central to my painting in every medium.

In many ways, the art of ethics as illustrated by this book is analogous to my painting of the magnolias. God has engaged us in a contract or agreement — a covenant — to live in relationship with God and one another. To be faithful to this agreement we require theological and ethical guidelines, which we create with the help of God's empowering presence.

Just as the painting for which I received a contract was for a specific room in a certain house, ethics is done by Christians for their particular settings. A church in an inner city needs a different ethical creation than a church in suburbia; Christians in Latin America or Africa or Asia have need of different ethics than do Christians in North America and Europe.

In the same way that I chose pigments to match a specific room, when we do the art of Christian ethics we must choose resources for our work that match the situation for which the ethics is being created. This assures us that the ethical guidelines we create are fitting for the particular place, people, and time for which they are intended. For the ethics of this book, derived largely out of and for the crises I dealt with in public health, the resources have been not only my life experiences as woman, artist, mother, and nurse, but also the writings of women from around the world. As a woman whose work was primarily with women and their families, I found that feminist and third-world women's perspectives were the fitting resources to match the situations for which I was creating theology and ethics.

The creation of ethics is done in and for actual life situations and must reflect the realities of those situations. Just as I had to seek out numerous blooming branches of magnolia trees to be sure my rendition of them was realistic, so we have to know the realities that surround the situations for which we do ethics. Major sections of part 2 have been devoted to this important ethical work of seeing the realities.

The art of ethics that we Christians create is not always acceptable to conventional ways of thinking. Those who have not been part of the creative processes may be startled or offended, just as the physician was when I first delivered the painting to her. I recall an anecdote reported by a member of a church task force on sexuality. Based on an ethic of love firmly grounded in scripture, this task force arrived at an inclusive stance that embraced both heterosexual and homosexual persons in committed relationships outside of marriage. One faithful Christian and devoted church leader was heard to remark: "We've got to decide whether we're going to be loving or moral." The ethic of the task force was so unconventional to her that she could not accept it as Christian morality. Ethics created for new times, places, and circumstances always will be unconventional and often will be controversial.

Ethics as the art of faithful Christians is done with both passion and reason, emotions and research, concern and rhetoric. If there is no joy or anguish or fear or sense of risk — all emotions that drive us to action — then we will not do Christian ethics. As an artist of paintings and an author of ethics, I cannot imagine expending so much time and energy on researching and executing a work without passionate concern about the impact that it will have on those for whom it is created. Neither will we as Christians be motivated to find faithful ways to respond to God and one another in the crises and dilemmas of our particular times and places if we do not care passionately about the results, about the impact that our ethical art will have.

My fervent hope is that readers will find in this work of ethics unconventional mirrors in which to see Christian life and reflect on the particular social crises I have addressed. But my impassioned prayer is that readers will find in this work insights into how you, in communities of the faithful, might create Christian ethics in relation to the social crises and the moral questions that are intense concerns of your life situations. If we as Christians care passionately about our life together in this world, there is much ethical thinking and moral acting to be done.

Appendix

Questions for Reflection and Discussion

Chapter 1: UNCONVENTIONAL MIRRORS

1. This book uses *unconventional* mirrors of women in which to see human life and social crises. What is your understanding of *conventional* Christian (or religious) mirrors in which we see our lives and world? What aspects of conventional views do you find most helpful for understanding and responding to the present time? Which are the least helpful?

2. What experiences that are unique to women can function as sources for doing theology and ethics?

3. Would a Christian worldview based entirely on women's experiences and corresponding perceptions be more, equally, or less adequate than a Christianity built entirely on men's experiences and corresponding perceptions?

4. Why is it necessary to reformulate Christian understandings of God and human life for new times and new settings? In what ways does this weaken or strengthen Christian teachings about faithful moral behavior?

5. Have you ever been motivated to do something significant in addressing a social need (or moral problem) without first feeling passionately concerned about it?

6. Can you think of an instance in which a law or code required you to do something of deep moral significance? What was the feeling behind your behavior?

7. Can we act morally and responsibly without both passion and reason? Explain.

Chapter 2: PAINTING

1. In this chapter painting is used as a metaphor to think about all kinds of human and divine creativity. What creative experiences have you

had that help you understand God's creative work in our world and God's gift of creativity to human beings?

2. Why have Christians usually spoken of God in terms of a person (or persons)?

3. What problems arise from using either maternal or paternal language to speak of God?

4. Conventional Christianity has shied away from using language related to women's reproductive creativity to speak about God and faith. Why do you think this has been the case?

5. What have been the consequences of ignoring women's reproductive experiences in formulating Christian ideas and beliefs? Has Christianity been more or less relevant to the lived realities of our day-to-day existence because of this?

6. What can we human beings do to exercise our transcending creativity in ways that do not cause circumstances that might harm life?

7. In this chapter human freedom is understood as the ability to create life and transcend barriers to life; that is, we have thought about freedom *for* rather than freedom *from* life/relationships/responsibility. Compare this view of freedom to other Christian teachings and philosophical ideas about human freedom.

Chapter 3: COOKING

1. Think about your last meal. How many people, in which places and over what period of time, were needed in order that you could eat that meal? How are you dependent on those people? How are they dependent on you?

2. What problems arise when we think of God as dependent on human acts? What problems arise when we think of God as wholly independent of human acts?

3. If God does not need human beings, why were we created? What is our purpose for being? What do we mean by Christian ministry or mission?

4. Think of some of the times you have been dependent on others for your well-being or your very life. How did these experiences help you understand our need for others on whom we can depend?

5. Can you recall times when you needed to depend on others for your well-being and did not find anyone to meet your needs? How did this feel?

6. Can you think of situations in which being forced to be dependent or choosing to be dependent on others would be dehumanizing?

7. In what ways have your understandings of what is right and wrong (or good and evil) been dependent on your interactions with others? Did your sense of right and wrong in relation to actual personal needs or concrete societal situations correspond with what you have been taught about Christian morality?

Chapter 4: QUILTING

1. In quilt making, the design, the materials, and the crafting all contribute to the quality of the finished product. What aspects of Christian life are analogous to each of these three components of quilting? How do they affect the quality of life?

2. Does the idea of God as co-quilter — that is, as a co-working and co-empowering one among us — weaken or strengthen the belief that we can depend upon God for all things? Why?

3. In this chapter God's empowering presence is found in the cooperative interactions of groups working for justice and mercy. Are there biblical bases for seeing God's work in human history in this way? If so, what are they?

4. Is it more or less difficult to see God in social interactions and political affairs than in personal meditation or mystical experiences? How has God been revealed to you?

5. In this chapter the "kingdom of God" — reinterpreted to mean the "empowerment of God" — is understood as means rather than end (as tool rather than product). What changes occur in your way of thinking about God and human history when kingdom language is replaced by the idea of empowerment?

6. If Jesus' kingdom sayings mean God's empowerment of human beings instead of God's reign over human history, what faith response is involved?

7. To think of Christian ethics in terms of moral destiny as well as moral acts means that the Christian life has to do with the future as well as the present, with institutional forms as well as social interaction, with the political as well as the personal. Are there ever times when a future, institutional, or political goal requires (or allows) actions that are immoral from a contemporary and individual perspective? Explain.

Chapter 5: WEAVING

1. In this chapter we have seen that different understandings of power emerge when transcending creativity, dependence, and cooperation are woven together. Do you see other moral understandings at the intersections of these same strands of human life?

2. Are there other forms of power not included in this chapter? What are they? How do they relate to the kinds of power included here?

3. Give positive and negative illustrations of controlling power (authority); persuasive power (influence); midwifery power (empowerment).

4. What are the sources of power? Are the sources of power, or the uses of power, more determinative of power's moral status?

5. Does any one form of power have moral significance without the others? Can any one of them have social impact without the others?

6. If theology and ethics arise out of particular personal needs and social circumstances, how can they have any validity or authority for other Christians?

7. Why is it impossible for persons from one social setting or life situation to speak authentically for or to persons from another setting or situation? Is there any connection between this question and the preceding one? How do these two questions relate to question 4 for chapter 1, regarding the need to reformulate Christian ethics for new times and new settings?

Chapter 6: WELFARE

1. Other than a problematic welfare system, what *social* ramifications result from our failure to value women's work of bearing and rearing children or providing other nurture and care in the home?

2. What are the *economic* repercussions of failure to pay for nurturing work in one's own home or to provide Social Security credit for such labor? Why is this a greater issue today than it was a generation ago? A century ago?

3. What options do poor parents have within our present socioeconomic structures to provide adequately for themselves and their children?

4. What changes in our socioeconomic structures would be necessary to make it possible for poor families to care for their dependent children adequately?

5. Pick ten professions or jobs and rank them in order of their social importance and monetary value. Where would you place the work of mothers in relation to this list?

6. Imagine what our nation would be like if care-giving roles were both prepared for and compensated for on the basis of their social and economic value to society.

7. If the work of bearing and rearing children were valued and compensated like other work that contributes to our society's well-being, how would it change our education system? Our work force?

Chapter 7: REPRODUCTIVE CHOICES

1. Over the years polls have shown that most Americans are both antiabortion and pro-choice. Is this a contradiction?

2. In what ways do our understandings of reproductive science affect our moral views about abortion? Have these changed over the years?

3. The Bible does not address the question of abortion directly. Why do you think this is the case?

4. If we had a pro-life society, as defined in this chapter, would the legal right for abortion still be necessary? Why?

5. Is it morally right to bear a child in social or economic circumstances that prevent a good life? Why?

6. Under what, if any, circumstances should the government have power over women's reproductive choices?

7. What impact does the legal status of abortion have on religious thinking and moral choices related to abortion?

Chapter 8: ADDICTION

1. Tobacco, alcohol, and cocaine (and other legal and illegal addictive substances) are all drugs that harm individual users, their families and associates, and society. Should they all have the same moral status? The same legal status?

2. Tobacco, alcohol, and cocaine (and other legal and illegal addictive substances) all contribute to our economy in various ways. What would be the socioeconomic ramifications of banning all of them? Of legalizing and controlling all of them?

3. What are some of the social pressures and conditions that encourage drug use? How do these vary in different socioeconomic settings?

4. What social and economic changes are needed to reduce the use of addictive drugs?

5. What social conditions and cultural attitudes are most likely to help people in overcoming their addictions? Which are likely to hinder?

6. In chapter 3, dependence is seen as the root reality of being human. How does this understanding of our humanity affect the way we think about the emotional and physical dependence of addiction?

7. Give some specific examples of ways in which drug addiction prevents individuals from living out their full humanity. How does addiction affect the drug-impaired persons, their families, their employers and co-workers, and social institutions?

Chapter 9: HANDICAPPING CONDITIONS

1. How does the language used to speak about persons with disabilities affect the way others think and feel about them? How does it affect the way they feel and think about themselves?

2. Why do many people fear, avoid, or denigrate persons who have handicapping conditions?

3. Why do some people tend to think of persons with disabilities as less than human?

4. What are some of the positive and negative impacts of using government regulations to determine how persons living with disabilities are to be treated?

5. What safeguards are necessary to insure that legislation and/or programs for persons with handicapping conditions do not denigrate or exploit them?

6. What needs to be done in your communities of association (church, school, recreational facility, place of work) to make them physically accessible and socially hospitable to persons with handicapping conditions?

7. How is it possible to give an empowering handicap to one group without disempowering another? Can you think of instances when one group has been given opportunities that seemed to disadvantage another group? What were the dynamics?

Chapter 10: CATASTROPHIC DISEASES

1. Christians have responded in both constructive and destructive ways to the AIDS epidemic. What can we learn about Christian morality by the ways we have responded to the AIDS crisis?

2. HIV/AIDS is frightening because it is associated with both sex and death. How might we have responded to the disease if it were spread in other ways and were curable?

3. Christianity has tended to see life and death in opposition. As creatures of God, can we have life without death? As creatures in God's image, can we have life without death?

4. Christianity has tended to see spirituality and sexuality in opposition. As creatures of God, can we be fully human without embracing our sexuality in all its diversity?

5. In thinking about persons living with permanent disabilities, we saw that Jesus' healing ministry created difficulties for Christians. Does the incurable nature of HIV/AIDS evoke the same kind of questions for Christians?

6. AIDS puts all the social crises of our time in sharper focus; absent or deficient social structures that are needed to address other societal problems also are needed to address the AIDS epidemic. What specific systemic changes do you think are necessary in order to respond to the AIDS crisis in a moral way?

7. Give concrete examples of ways that (a) a moral imperative for life, based on transcending creativity, can address the AIDS crisis; (b) a morally positive view of dependence as the root reality of being human helps us meet the needs of persons living with HIV/AIDS; (c) a moral destiny of cooperation empowers a response to HIV/AIDS; and (d) different understandings of power affect our work with persons who have HIV/AIDS.

Notes

Chapter 1: UNCONVENTIONAL MIRRORS

1. Virginia Fabella and Mercy Amba Oduyoye, "Introduction," in *With Passion and Compassion: Third World Women Doing Theology*, ed. Virginia Fabella and Mercy Amba Oduyoye (Maryknoll, N.Y.: Orbis Books, 1988), ix.

2. Beverly Wildung Harrison, "The Power of Anger in the Work of Love: Christian Ethics for Women and Other Strangers," in Beverly Wildung Harrison, *Making the Connections: Essays in Feminist Social Ethics*, ed. Carol S. Robb (Boston: Beacon Press, 1985), 3–21.

3. Bärbel von Wartenberg-Potter, *We Will Not Hang Our Harps on the Willows: Global Sisterhood and God's Song*, trans. Fred Kaan (Geneva: WCC Publications, 1987; Oak Park, Ill.: Meyer-Stone Books, 1988), 1, 2.

4. Ibid., 2

5. Chung Hyun Kyung, " 'Han-pu-ri': Doing Theology from Korean Women's Perspective," in *We Dare to Dream: Doing Theology as Asian Women*, ed. Virginia Fabella and Sun Ai Lee Park (Hong Kong: Asian Women's Resource Centre for Culture, 1989; Manila: Asian Office of the Women's Commission of the Ecumenical Association of Third World Theologians, 1989; Maryknoll, N.Y.: Orbis Books, 1990), 144.

6. Fabella and Oduyoye, "Final Document: Intercontinental Women's Conference," in *With Passion and Compassion*, ed. Fabella and Oduyoye, 188.

Chapter 2: PAINTING

1. See Mary John Mananzan and Sun Ai Park, "Emerging Spirituality of Asian Women," in *With Passion and Compassion: Third World Women Doing Theology*, ed. Virginia Fabella and Mercy Amba Oduyoye (Maryknoll, N.Y.: Orbis Books, 1988), 81.

2. See Aruna Gnanadason, "Women's Oppression: A Sinful Situation," in *With Passion and Compassion*, ed. Fabella and Oduyoye, 69–73; and Mananzan and Park, "Emerging Spirituality," 78–79, 82–83.

3. Sallie McFague, *Models of God: Theology for an Ecological, Nuclear Age* (Philadelphia: Fortress Press, 1987), 103.

4. Ibid., 105.

5. Luz Beatriz Arellano, "Women's Experience of God in Emerging Spirituality," in *With Passion and Compassion*, ed. Fabella and Oduyoye, 141–42, 141.

6. Mercy Amba Oduyoye, *Hearing and Knowing: Theological Reflections on Christianity in Africa* (Maryknoll, N.Y.: Orbis Books, 1986), 136, 137.

7. Presbyterian Church (U.S.A.), *Covenant and Creation: Theological Reflections on Contraception and Abortion* (Louisville, Ky.: Office of the General Assembly, Presbyterian Church, 1983), 37.

8. Beverly Wildung Harrison, "The Power of Anger in the Work of Love: Christian Ethics for Women and Other Strangers," in Beverly Wildung Harrison, *Making the Connections: Essays in Feminist Social Ethics*, ed. Carol S. Robb (Boston: Beacon Press, 1985), 12.

9. Reinhold Niebuhr, *The Nature and Destiny of Man*, vol. 1: *Human Nature* (reprint; New York: Charles Scribner's Sons, 1964.)

10. McFague, *Models of God*, 106.

11. Ibid., 110.

12. Nelle Morton, *The Journey Is Home* (Boston: Beacon Press, 1985), 90–91.

13. Carter Heyward, *Our Passion for Justice: Images of Power, Sexuality, and Liberation* (New York: Pilgrim Press, 1984), 245.

14. Judith Groch, *The Right to Create* (Boston: Little, Brown & Co., 1969), 52.

15. See Susan Brooks Thistlethwaite, " 'I Am Become Death': God in the Nuclear Age," in *Lift Every Voice: Constructing Theology from the Underside*, ed. Susan Brooks Thistlethwaite and Mary Potter Engel (San Francisco: Harper & Row, 1990), 96.

16. Letty M. Russell, *Human Liberation in a Feminist Perspective — A Theology* (Philadelphia: Westminster Press, 1974), 25–32.

Chapter 3: COOKING

1. Grace Eneme, "Living Stones," in *New Eyes for Reading: Biblical and Theological Reflections by Women from the Third World*, ed. John S. Pobee and Bärbel von Wartenberg-Potter (Geneva: WCC Publications, 1986), 28.

2. Ibid.

3. Phyllis Trible, *God and the Rhetoric of Sexuality*, Overtures to Biblical Theology series (Philadelphia: Fortress Press, 1978), 90.

4. Elizabeth Dodson Gray, "Eden's Garden Revisited: A Christian Ecological Perspective," in *With Both Eyes Open: Seeing Beyond Gender*, ed. Patricia Altenbernd Johnson and Janet Kalven (New York: Pilgrim Press, 1988), 52.

5. Beverly Wildung Harrison, "The Power of Anger in the Work of Love: Christian Ethics for Women and Other Strangers," in Beverly Wildung Harrison, *Making the Connections: Essays in Feminist Social Ethics*, ed. Carol S. Robb (Boston: Beacon Press, 1985), 16.

6. Sharon D. Welch, *A Feminist Ethic of Risk* (Minneapolis: Fortress Press, 1990), 159–60.

7. Paul Tillich, *The Courage to Be* (New Haven and London: Yale University Press, 1952).

8. Welch, *Feminist Ethic of Risk*, 160.

9. Carter Heyward, *Touching Our Strength: The Erotic as Power and the Love of God* (San Francisco: Harper & Row, 1989), 21–22.

10. Jacquelyn Grant, *White Women's Christ and Black Women's Jesus: Feminist Christology and Womanist Response* (Atlanta: Scholars Press, 1989), 216.

11. Louise Tappa, "The Christ-Event from the Viewpoint of African Women: A Protestant Perspective," in *With Passion and Compassion: Third World Women Doing*

Theology, ed. Virginia Fabella and Mercy Amba Oduyoye (Maryknoll, N.Y.: Orbis Books, 1988), 33.

12. Thérèsa Souga, "The Christ-Event from the Viewpoint of African Women: A Catholic Perspective," in *With Passion and Compassion*, ed. Fabella and Oduyoye, 28.

13. Ibid., 29.

14. María Teresa Porcile S., "Water in the Slums," in *New Eyes for Reading*, ed. Pobee and Wartenberg-Potter, 33, 34.

15. Mary Potter Engel, "Evil, Sin, and Violation of the Vulnerable," in *Lift Every Voice: Constructing Theology from the Underside*, ed. Susan Brooks Thistlethwaite and Mary Potter Engel (San Francisco: Harper & Row, 1990), 162.

16. Ibid., 163.

17. Bärbel von Wartenberg-Potter, *We Will Not Hang Our Harps on the Willows: Global Sisterhood and God's Song*, trans. Fred Kaan (Geneva: WCC Publications, 1987; Oak Park, Ill.: Meyer-Stone Books, 1988), 52.

18. John Rawls, *A Theory of Justice* (Cambridge, Mass.: Belknap Press, 1971).

Chapter 4: QUILTING

1. *Quilts in Women's Lives, Six Portraits*, videorecording from Ferrero Films; producer-director Pat Ferrero, San Francisco. Distributed by New Day Films, New York. 1980.

2. Pat Hoffman, "AIDS Quilt: A Church to Call Home," *Christianity and Crisis* 50 (December 17, 1990): 397.

3. Academy of Medicine of New Jersey, *AIDSline* 4 (August 1992): 2.

4. Hoffman, "AIDS Quilt," 397.

5. Ibid., 397–98.

6. Nelle Morton, *The Journey Is Home* (Boston: Beacon Press, 1985), 54–55.

7. *Webster's New Collegiate Dictionary* (1981), s.v. "cooperate."

8. Rita Nakashima Brock, *Journeys by Heart: A Christology of Erotic Power* (New York: Crossroad, 1988).

9. Alida Verhoeven, "The Concept of God: A Feminine Perspective," in *Through Her Eyes: Women's Theology from Latin America*, ed. Elsa Tamez (Maryknoll, N.Y.: Orbis Books, 1989), 51–52; my emphases.

10. Ibid., 54.

11. Beverly Wildung Harrison, in the Mudflower Collective, *God's Fierce Whimsy: Christian Feminism and Theological Education* (New York: Pilgrim Press, 1985), 112.

12. Sallie McFague, *Models of God: Theology for an Ecological, Nuclear Age* (Philadelphia: Fortress Press, 1987), 179.

13. Letty M. Russell, *Becoming Human* (Philadelphia: Westminster Press, 1982), 45.

14. Ibid., 45–46.

15. Ada María Isasi-Díaz, "Solidarity: Love of Neighbor in the 1980s," in *Lift Every Voice: Constructing Theology from the Underside*, ed. Susan Brooks Thistlethwaite and Mary Potter Engel (San Francisco: Harper & Row, 1990), 304 n. 4.

16. Sharon D. Welch, *A Feminist Ethic of Risk* (Minneapolis: Fortress Press, 1990), 160–61.

17. Elizabeth Domínguez, "New Testament Reflections on Political Power," in *New Eyes for Reading: Biblical and Theological Reflections by Women from the Third World,* ed. John S. Pobee and Bärbel von Wartenberg-Potter (Geneva: WCC Publications, 1986), 47.

18. Sharon H. Ringe, *Jesus, Liberation, and the Biblical Jubilee: Images for Ethics and Christology* (Philadelphia: Fortress Press, 1985), 4.

19. Ibid.

20. Carter Heyward, *Touching Our Strength: The Erotic as Power and the Love of God* (San Francisco: Harper & Row, 1989), 73.

21. Ibid.

22. Chung Hyun Kyung, *Struggle to Be the Sun Again: Introducing Asian Women's Theology* (Maryknoll, N.Y.: Orbis Books, 1990), 39.

23. Ibid., 101; citing Lee Sung Hee, "Women's Liberation Theology as the Foundation for Asian Theology," *East Asian Journal of Theology* 4 (October 1986): 12–13. Brackets ([hu]mankind) are Chung's.

24. Virginia Fabella and Sun Ai Lee Park, "Introduction," in *We Dare to Dream: Doing Theology as Asian Women,* ed. Virginia Fabella and Sun Ai Lee Park (Hong Kong: Asian Women's Resource Centre for Culture, 1989; Manila: Asian Office of the Women's Commission of the Ecumenical Association of Third World Theologians, 1989; Maryknoll, N.Y.: Orbis Books, 1990), x.

25. Welch, *Feminist Ethic of Risk,* 3.

26. Rosemary Radford Ruether, "Eschatology and Feminism," in *Lift Every Voice,* ed. Thistlethwaite and Engel, 121.

27. Rosemary Radford Ruether, "Envisioning Our Hopes: Some Models for the Future," in *Women's Spirit Bonding,* ed. Janet Kalven and Mary I. Buckley (New York: Pilgrim Press, 1984), 335.

Chapter 5: WEAVING

1. Sharon D. Welch, *A Feminist Ethic of Risk* (Minneapolis: Fortress Press, 1990), 116, 118.

2. Chung Hyun Kyung, *Struggle to Be the Sun Again: Introducing Asian Women's Theology* (Maryknoll, N.Y.: Orbis Books, 1990), 51.

3. Ibid. Chung cites in poetic form prose by Chitra Fernando, "Towards a Theology Related to a Full Humanity," *In God's Image* (April 1985): 24.

4. Susan Brooks Thistlethwaite and Mary Potter Engel, "Introduction to Part 5," in *Lift Every Voice: Constructing Theology from the Underside,* ed. Susan Brooks Thistlethwaite and Mary Potter Engel (San Francisco: Harper & Row, 1990), 167.

5. Crescy John, "Woman and the Holy Spirit: From an Indian Perspective," in *We Dare to Dream: Doing Theology as Asian Women,* ed. Virginia Fabella and Sun Ai Lee Park (Hong Kong: Asian Women's Resource Centre for Culture, 1989; Manila: Asian Office of the Women's Commission of the Ecumenical Association of Third World Theologians, 1989; Maryknoll, N.Y.: Orbis Books, 1990), 61.

6. María Clara Bingemer, "Reflections on the Trinity," in *Through Her Eyes: Women's Theology from Latin America,* ed. Elsa Tamez (Maryknoll, N.Y.: Orbis Books,

1989), 75–76. She cites Elisabeth Moltmann-Wendel and Jürgen Moltmann, *Dieu, homme et femme* (Paris: Cerf, 1984), 136.

7. Carter Heyward, *Our Passion for Justice: Images of Power, Sexuality, and Liberation* (New York: Pilgrim Press, 1984), 117.

8. Carter Heyward, *Touching Our Strength: The Erotic as Power and the Love of God* (San Francisco: Harper & Row, 1989), 66.

9. Bärbel von Wartenberg-Potter, *We Will Not Hang Our Harps on the Willows: Global Sisterhood and God's Song*, trans. Fred Kaan (Geneva: WCC Publications, 1987; Oak Park, Ill.: Meyer-Stone Books, 1988), 118–19.

10. Anna Case-Winter, *God's Power: Traditional Understandings and Contemporary Challenges* (Louisville, Ky.: Westminster/John Knox Press, 1990), 201.

11. Ibid., 212.

12. Rita Nakashima Brock, *Journeys by Heart: A Christology of Erotic Power* (New York: Crossroad, 1988), 34.

13. Ibid.

14. Amanda Mayer Stenchecum, "Tartans Galore in Scotland," *New York Times*, July 19, 1992, sec. 5.

Chapter 6: WELFARE

1. Rosemary Haughton, "The Economics of the Dispossessed," *Religion and Intellectual Life* 4 (Fall 1986): 26–27.

2. Pamela Sparr, "Reevaluating Feminist Economics: 'Feminization of Poverty' Ignores Key Issues," in *For Crying Out Loud: Women and Poverty in the United States*, ed. Rochelle Lefkowitz and Ann Withorn (New York: Pilgrim Press, 1986), 61.

3. Mimi Abramovitz, "Welfare, Work, and Women: How 'Welfare Reform' Is Turning Back the Clock," *Christianity and Crisis* 48 (September 12, 1988): 293.

4. Elaine Donovan and Mary Huff Stevenson, "Shortchanged: The Political Economy of Women's Poverty," in *For Crying Out Loud*, ed. Lefkowitz and Withorn, 53.

5. Barbara Ehrenreich, "What Makes Women Poor?" in *For Crying Out Loud*, ed. Lefkowitz and Withorn, 20.

6. Abramovitz, "Welfare, Work, and Women," 296.

7. Haughton, "Economics of the Dispossessed," 23–25.

8. Nancy Bancroft, "Women in the Cutback Economy: Ethics, Ideology, and Class," in *Women's Consciousness, Women's Conscience: A Reader in Feminist Ethics*, ed. Barbara Hilkert Andolsen, Christine E. Gudorf, and Mary D. Pellauer (San Francisco: Harper & Row, 1985), 20.

9. Haughton, "Economics of the Dispossessed," 27.

10. Ehrenreich, "What Makes Women Poor?" 21–22.

11. My own observations on this are supported by the work of Nancy Aries, "Teenage Mothers: Seduced and Abandoned," in *For Crying Out Loud*, ed. Lefkowitz and Withorn, 126.

12. Abramovitz, "Welfare, Work, and Women," 295.

13. *New York Times*, Sunday, July 26, 1992, national section.

14. Theresa Funiciello, "Welfare Mothers Earn Their Way," *Christianity and Crisis* 44 (December 10, 1984): 469.

15. *All of Our Lives,* a videorecording from Filmmakers Library, Inc., 1984.

16. Funiciello, "Welfare Mothers Earn Their Way," 473.

17. Ibid., 470.

18. Ibid., 470–71.

19. Abramovitz, "Women, Work, and Welfare," 294–95 (see box).

20. Funiciello, "Welfare Mothers Earn Their Way," 469–70.

21. Anonymous, "Freedom Is Not Having to Sell Ass," in *My Story's On! Ordinary Women/Extraordinary Lives,* ed. Paula Ross (Berkeley, Calif.: Common Differences Press, 1985), 14–15.

22. Arlene Eisen, "Mother Pride," in *My Story's On,* ed. Ross, 8–9.

23. Ibid., 9.

24. Ibid., 10.

25. Abramovitz, "Women, Work, and Welfare," 294–95 (see box).

26. Ibid., 296.

27. Betty Reid Mandell, "Welfare: Death by Exhaustion," in *For Crying Out Loud,* ed. Lefkowitz and Withorn, 190–210.

28. *Living below the Line,* a videorecording from PBS, 1984.

29. Ann Withorn, "For Better and for Worse: Women against Women in the Welfare State," in *For Crying Out Loud,* ed. Lefkowitz and Withorn, 220–34.

30. See also *Gentle Angry People,* a videorecording, Catholic Charities, USA, 1986.

31. Haughton, "Economics of the Dispossessed," 23, 25.

32. Diane Dujon, Judy Gradford, and Dottie Stevens, "Reports from the Front: Welfare Mothers Up in Arms," in *For Crying Out Loud,* ed. Lefkowitz and Withorn, 216.

33. Ibid., 218.

34. Haughton, "Economics of the Dispossessed," 24.

35. Dujon, Gradford, and Stevens, "Reports from the Front," 217–18.

36. Ibid., 212.

37. Haughton, "Economics of the Dispossessed," 25.

38. Teresa Amott and Julie Matthaei, "Comparable Worth, Incomparable Pay," in *For Crying Out Loud,* ed. Lefkowitz and Withorn, 316–25.

39. Frances Fox Piven, "Women and the State: Ideology, Power, and Welfare," in *For Crying Out Loud,* ed. Lefkowitz and Withorn, 326–40.

40. Roberta Praeger, "A World Worth Living In," in *For Crying Out Loud,* ed. Lefkowitz and Withorn, 89–98.

41. Teresa Amott and Pat Jerabek, "Learning for a Change: The Role of Critical Economics Education," in *For Crying Out Loud,* ed. Lefkowitz and Withorn, 275–84.

42. Deanne Bonnar, "Towards the Feminization of Policy: Exit from an Ancient Trap by the Redefinition of Work," in *For Crying Out Loud,* ed. Lefkowitz and Withorn, 285–99.

Chapter 7: REPRODUCTIVE CHOICES

1. Le Anne Schreiber, "What Kind of Abortions Do We Want?" *New York Times Book Review* (January 13, 1993): 13.

2. Julie Johnson, Priscilla Painton, and Elizabeth Taylor, "Abortion: The Future Is Already Here," *Time* (May 4, 1992): 26–32.

3. Schreiber, "What Kind of Abortions," 13–14.

4. See Beverly Wildung Harrison, *Our Right to Choose: Toward a New Ethic of Abortion* (Boston: Beacon Press, 1983).

5. In contrast, see Beverly Harrison and Mary Lou Suhor in "A Conversation with Beverly Harrison: The Politics of Reproduction," *Witness* 72 (June 1989): 12–14.

6. Susan Power Bratton, *Six Billion & More: Human Population Regulation and Christian Ethics* (Louisville, Ky.: Westminster/John Knox Press, 1992), 80–81.

7. Ibid., 81–85.

8. Faye Wattleton, "Reproductive Rights are *Fundamental* Rights," *Humanist* 51 (January–February 1991): 21, 42.

9. Bratton, *Six Billion & More,* chapters 4 and 6–8.

10. See Virginia Ramey Mollenkott, "Reproductive Choice: Basic to Justice for Women," *Christian Scholar's Review* 17, no. 3 (1988): 286–87.

11. Charles F. Westoff and Jane S. DeLung, "Abortions Preventable by Contraceptive Practice," *Family Planning Perspectives* (September–October 1981): 218; cited in Presbyterian Church (U.S.A.), *Covenant and Creation: Theological Reflections on Contraception and Abortion* (Louisville, Ky.: Office of the General Assembly, Presbyterian Church, 1983), 33.

12. Robert A. Hatcher, *Contraceptive Technology 1980–1981* (New York: Irvington Publishers, Inc., 1981), 4; cited in Presbyterian Church (U.S.A.), *Covenant and Creation,* 33.

13. Faye Wattleton and Elizabeth Maxwell, "Planned Parenthood Head Calls on Churches to Support Choice," *Witness* 72 (June 1989): 8.

14. Carol Gilligan, "A Different Voice in Moral Decisions," in *Speaking of Faith: Cross-cultural Perspectives on Women, Religion and Social Change,* ed. Diane L. Eck and Devaki Jain (London: Women's Press, 1986), 223.

15. Ibid., 224.

16. See Mollenkott, "Reproductive Choice," 291.

17. Beverly W. Harrison, "A Theology of Pro-Choice: A Feminist Perspective on Abortion," in *Speaking of Faith,* ed. Eck and Jain, 205–6. See also Harrison, *Our Right to Choose,* especially chapters 2 and 8.

18. "Abortion Foes See Pivotal Voting Role," *New York Times,* June 13, 1992.

19. Terri P. Guess, "Quiet Cries," *Sunday Star-Ledger,* June 14, 1992, sec. 6.

20. See Barbara B. Blum and Susan Blank, "Children's Services in an Era of Budget Deficits," in *Caring for the Uninsured and Underinsured: A Compendium from JAMA and the Specialty Journals of the American Medical Association* (Chicago: American Medical Association, 1991), 36–39.

21. Harrison and Suhor, "A Conversation with Beverly Harrison," 13.

22. Julie Kosterlitz, "A Sick System," *National Journal* (February 15, 1992): 385.

23. Emily Friedman, "The Uninsured: From Dilemma to Crisis," in *Caring for the Uninsured and Underinsured,* J19.

24. Kosterlitz, "A Sick System," 376.

25. Katherine Hancock Ragsdale, "Legislative and Pastoral Implications: The Episcopal Church and Abortion," *Witness* 72 (June 1989): 20.

26. Sallie McFague, *Models of God: Theology for an Ecological, Nuclear Age* (Philadelphia: Fortress Press, 1987), 103.

27. Bratton, *Six Billion & More*, 133–36.

28. Sidney Callahan, "Abortion and the Sexual Agenda," in *Moral Issues and Christian Response*, ed. Paul T. Jersild and Dale A. Johnson, 4th ed. (New York: Holt, Rinehart & Winston, 1988), 368–73.

29. Harrison, "A Theology of Pro-Choice," 202.

30. "Excerpts from the Justices' Decision in the Pennsylvania Case," *New York Times*, June 30, 1992, sec. A.

31. See Mollenkott, "Reproductive Choice," 292–93.

32. See Patricia Wilson-Kastner, "Woman vs. Womb: Whose 'Life' Counts?" *Witness* 72 (June 1989): 21–22.

Chapter 8: ADDICTION

1. Anne Wilson Schaef, *When Society Becomes an Addict* (San Francisco: Harper & Row, 1987), 18.

2. Ibid., 16–17.

3. Eva Bertram, "It's Worth the Risk!" *Christian Social Action* 3 (June 1990): 11.

4. Lelia V. Hall and Dolores Finger Wright, "Alcohol and Drug Abuse among Women in Childbearing Years," *Engage/Social Action* 5 (November 1977): 43.

5. Susan L. Nelson, "Dysfunctional Families: Schools for Sin?" *Church and Society* 82 (May-June 1992): 13–18. Vol. 82 is entitled *A Body Broken: Substance Abuse and the Church*.

6. Jane Searjeant Watt, "The Feminine Face of Addiction," *Church and Society* 82 (May-June 1992): 39–40.

7. Sharon Zalewski, "Prescription Drug Addicts: Reflection of Social Ills," *Engage/Social Action* 3 (July-August 1985): 4–7.

8. Elaine M. Johnson, "Women's Health: Issues in Mental Health, Alcoholism, and Substance Abuse: Substance Abuse and Women's Health," *Public Health Reports* (supplement to the July-August 1987 issue): 42–47.

9. Watt, "Feminine Face of Addiction," 35–41.

10. Marsha Lillie-Blanton, Ellen MacKenzie, and James C. Anthony, "Black-White Differences in Alcohol Use by Women: Baltimore Survey Findings," *Public Health Reports* 106 (March-April 1991): 124.

11. Ibid.

12. Ibid., 130.

13. Jacqueline Berrien, "Pregnancy and Drug Use: Incarceration Is Not the Answer," in *From Abortion to Reproductive Freedom: Transforming a Movement*, ed. Marlene Gerber Fried (Boston: South End Press, 1990), 263.

14. Ibid., 264.

15. Ibid., 265–66, 265.

16. Eva Bertram and Robin Crawford, "Is the Drug War a Just War? Drug Abuse, Drug Wars, and the Church," *Church and Society* 82 (May-June 1992): 55–56.

17. Mary Nilsen, "But He's Not a Junkie!" *Other Side* (October 1982): 42.

18. Ibid., 43.

19. Bertram and Crawford, "Is the Drug War a Just War?" 62.

20. Ibid., 64.

21. Ibid., 55–57.

22. Methodist bishop Felton May at a National Council of Churches's Prophetic Justice Unit consultation, October 19, 1990, as reported by Sarah J. Vilankulu, "Churches Uniting against Drugs," *Christian Century* 107 (November 14, 1990): 1052.

23. Bertram, "It's Worth the Risk!" 13.

24. Ibid., 11–12.

25. Bertram and Crawford, "Is the Drug War a Just War?" 57–58.

26. Ibid., 52, 54.

27. Schaef, *When Society Is an Addict*, 19.

28. Ibid., 20.

29. In 1992 the Bush administration was promoting and piloting a drug-response program called "Weed and Seed"; this program has the advantage of not being a quick-fix. The "weed" aspect is law enforcement efforts; the "seed" aspect provides for some of the services needed in inner-city areas where the drug economy is a major problem. This program may not survive in today's political climate, but it does seem to recognize that more than interdiction is needed. Missing from the "seed" part of the program, however, are drug treatment centers and adequate attention to job training, education, and employment opportunities.

30. Bertram, "It's Worth the Risk!" 13.

Chapter 9: HANDICAPPING CONDITIONS

1. Connie Myer, "International Dimensions of Disability," *Witness* 64 (August 1981): 14.

2. See Betty Medsger, "You, Too, Could Be Disabled," *Witness* 64 (August 1981): 6, 5.

3. Peter T. Kilborn, "Major Shift Likely as Law Bans Bias toward Disabled," *New York Times*, Sunday, July 19, 1992, national section.

4. Rutgers University Bureau of Economic Research, as reported in *Sunday Star Ledger*, July 19, 1992, sec. 1.

5. See, for example, the minority report on abortion that was presented at the 1992 General Assembly of the Presbyterian Church (U.S.A.), as reported in *Presbyterian Outlook* 174 (June 22, 1992): 4.

6. Adrienne Asch and Michelle Fine, "Shared Dreams: A Left Perspective on Disability Rights and Reproductive Rights," in *From Abortion to Reproductive Freedom: Transforming a Movement*, ed. Marlene Gerber Fried (Boston: South End Press, 1990), 234, 238.

7. Meryn Stuart and Glynis Ellerington, "Unequal Access: Disabled Women's Exclusion from the Mainstream Women's Movement," *Women and Environments* 12 (Spring 1990): 18.

8. Nasa Begum, "Disabled Women and the Feminist Agenda," *Feminist Review* 40 (Spring 1992): 71.

9. Medsger, "You, Too, Could Be Disabled," 4–5.

10. Begum, "Disabled Women," 78.

11. Cited in Stuart and Ellerington, "Unequal Access," 18.

12. Gloria Maxson, " 'Whose Life Is It, Anyway?' Ours, That's Whose!" *Christian Century* 99 (October 20, 1982): 1039.

13. Begum, "Disabled Women," 78.

14. Ibid., 78–79.

15. Bonita A. Raine, "Sexuality and the Disabled Christian," in *The Church and Disabled Persons*, ed. Griff Hogan (Springfield, Ill.: Templegate Publishers, 1983), 33.

16. Betty Moore, "Outside the Camp," *Engage/Social Action* 10 (January 1982): 52.

17. Ruth Dinkins Rowan, "Education: An Equal Opportunity for All?" *Engage/Social Action* 7 (January 1979): 22.

18. Medsger, "You, Too, Could Be Disabled," 5.

19. Donna Leusner, "Businesses Prepare to Comply with Law Banning Bias against Disabled," *Sunday Star-Ledger*, July 19, 1992, sec. 1.

20. Ibid.

21. Kilborn, "Major Shift Likely."

22. Leusner, "Businesses Prepare."

23. Kilborn, "Major Shift Likely."

24. Leusner, "Businesses Prepare."

25. Kilborn, "Major Shift Likely."

26. Ibid.

27. Myer, "International Dimensions of Disability," 15.

Chapter 10: CATASTROPHIC DISEASES

1. Information about HIV/AIDS, unless otherwise noted, is from *AIDSline* (1991–92), a monthly publication of the Academy of Medicine of New Jersey; *NJWAN NEWS* (1991–92), a quarterly publication of the New Jersey Women and AIDS Network; NJWAN quarterly conferences in 1991; and Ines Rieder and Patricia Ruppelt, eds., *AIDS: The Women* (Pittsburgh: Cleis Press, 1988).

2. Katherine Franke, "Turning Issues Upside Down," in *AIDS: The Women*, ed. Rieder and Ruppelt, 228.

3. *New York Times*, Sunday, June 28, 1992, sec. E.

4. Jennifer Brown, "Life and Death with Joan," and Margaret, "Living on Substances," in *AIDS: The Women*, ed. Rieder and Ruppelt, 57–62, 91–94.

5. *British Medical Journal*, as reported by the Academy of Medicine of New Jersey in *AIDSline* (May 1992).

6. Information in this paragraph has been compiled from the following sources: Cécile De Sweemer, "AIDS: The Global Crisis," in *AIDS Issues: Confronting the Challenge*, ed. David G. Hallman (New York: Pilgrim Press, 1989), 28–50. Helen Jackson, "A Hidden Phenomenon"; Marie Marthe Saint Cyr-Delpe, "Reaching within, Reaching Out"; and Laurie Garrett, "A Report from the Front Lines," in *AIDS: The Women*, ed. Rieder and Ruppelt, 205–10, 217–19, 198–201. *New York Times*, Sunday, June 28, 1992, sec. E.

7. Lawrence K. Altman, "Women Worldwide Nearing Higher Rate for AIDS than Men," *New York Times*, July 21, 1992, science section.

8. New Jersey Women and AIDS Network, "HIV Testing Concerns for Women," *NJWAN NEWS* (Summer 1992).

9. Franke, "Turning Issues Upside Down," 226.

10. Some of the most prevalent women-specific clusters of HIV diseases are: chronic and recurrent vaginal yeast infections, cervical cancer, pelvic inflammatory disease (PID), and other diseases of the pelvic reproductive organs and female genitalia. In January 1993, the CDC finally added cervical cancer to the list of maladies considered AIDS. Some of the CDC-defined disease complexes of AIDS, which can be found in all populations, are: pneumocystis carinii pneumonia (PCP), cytomegalovirus (CMV), and Kaposi's sarcoma (KS). Other frequently observed symptoms of AIDS include lymph node enlargement, fevers, night sweats, rapid weight loss, and persistent diarrhea.

11. *New York Times,* Sunday, June 28, 1992, sec. E.

12. Ines Rieder and Patricia Ruppelt, "Prostitution in the Age of AIDS," in *AIDS: The Women,* ed. Rieder and Ruppelt, 155–56.

13. Lynn Hampton, "Hookers with AIDS — the Search"; Priscilla Alexander, "A Chronology, of Sorts"; and Garrett, "Report from the Front Lines," in *AIDS: The Women,* ed. Rieder and Ruppelt, 157–64, 169–72, 194–98.

14. Tema Luft, "Going Public," in *AIDS: The Women,* ed. Rieder and Ruppelt, 65–70.

15. Saint Cyr-Delpe, "Reaching Within," 219.

16. Marion D. Banzhaf, Coordinator, New Jersey Women and AIDS Network. Written information presented to author, April 8, 1993.

17. Saint Cyr-Delpe, "Reaching Within," 217.

18. Hortensia Amaro, "Women's Reproductive Rights in the Age of AIDS: New Threats to Informed Choice," in *From Abortion to Reproductive Freedom,* ed. Fried, 253.

19. Ibid., 251–54.

20. Erik Eckholm, "Illness Can Be Delayed," *New York Times,* Sunday, June 28, 1992, sec. E.

21. Yolanda Serrano, "Crack Down on AIDS," in *AIDS: The Women,* ed. Rieder and Ruppelt, 116–17.

22. Naomi Schapiro, "AIDS Brigade: Organizing Prevention," in *AIDS: The Women,* ed. Rieder and Ruppelt, 211.

23. Amaro, "Women's Reproductive Rights," 246.

24. Ibid., 250.

25. J. Shannon Clarkson, ed., "Life Stories," in *The Church with AIDS: Renewal in the Midst of Crisis,* ed. Letty M. Russell (Louisville, Ky.: Westminster/John Knox Press, 1990), 156–57.

26. Rieder and Ruppelt, "Prostitution in the Age of AIDS," 155–56.

27. Lisa Berlin, "New Jersey Needs a Needle Exchange Program," *NJWAN NEWS* (Summer 1992): 7.

28. Erik Eckholm, "AIDS, Fatally Steady in the U.S., Accelerates Worldwide," *New York Times,* Sunday, June 28, 1992, sec. E.

29. Eckholm, "Illness Can Be Delayed."

30. Ilse Groth, "Bright Candles in the Dark," and Elisabeth, "Being Positive Is Positive," in *AIDS: The Women,* ed. Rieder and Ruppelt, 71–77, 81–87.

31. J. H., "Just Getting By," and D. R., "My Kids Keep Me Going," in *AIDS: The Women,* ed. Rieder and Ruppelt, 78–80, 95–100.

32. Abigail Zuger, "Professional Responsibilities in the AIDS Generation: AIDS on the Wards: A Residency in Medical Ethics," *Hastings Center Report* 17 (June 1987): 16–20.

33. Hedwig Bönsch, "Beyond the Call of Duty," and Deborah Stone, "A Selfish Kind of Giving," in *AIDS: The Women*, ed. Rieder and Ruppelt, 120–25, 143–50.

For Further Reading

Chapter 1: UNCONVENTIONAL MIRRORS

Belenky, Mary Field, et al., eds. *Women's Ways of Knowing: The Development of Self, Voice, and Mind.* New York: Basic Books, 1986.

Callahan, Sidney. *In Good Conscience: Reason and Emotion in Moral Decision Making.* San Francisco: HarperCollins, 1991.

Hooks, Bell. *Ain't I a Woman? Black Women and Feminism.* Boston: South End Press, 1981.

Isasi-Díaz, Ada María, and Yolanda Tarango. *Hispanic Women: Prophetic Voice in the Church: Toward a Hispanic Women's Liberation Theology/Mujer Hispana: Voz Profética en la Iglesia: Hacia una Teología de Liberación de la Mujer Hispana.* San Francisco: Harper & Row, 1988.

Katoppo, Marianne. *Compassionate and Free: An Asian Woman's Theology.* Maryknoll, N.Y.: Orbis Books, 1979.

MacHaffe, Barbara J. *Her Story: Women in Christian Tradition.* Philadelphia: Fortress Press, 1986.

Newsome, Carol A., and Sharon H. Ringe, eds. *The Women's Bible Commentary.* London: SPCK; Louisville, Ky.: Westminster/John Knox Press, 1992.

Ruddick, Sara. *Maternal Thinking: Toward a Politics of Peace.* Boston: Beacon Press, 1989.

Ruether, Rosemary, and Eleanor McLaughlin, eds. *Women of Spirit: Female Leadership in the Jewish and Christian Traditions.* New York: Simon and Schuster, 1979.

Russell, Letty M., ed. *Feminist Interpretation of the Bible.* Philadelphia: Westminster Press, 1985.

Russell, Letty M., et al., eds. *Inheriting Our Mothers' Gardens: Feminist Theology in Third World Perspective.* Philadelphia: Westminster Press, 1988.

Schüssler Fiorenza, Elisabeth. *But She Said: Feminist Practices of Biblical Interpretation.* Boston: Beacon Press, 1992.

———. *In Memory of Her: A Feminist Reconstruction of Christian Origins.* Boston: Beacon Press, 1985.

Smith, Dorothy E. *The Everyday World as Problematic: A Feminist Sociology.* Boston: Northeastern University Press, 1987.

Spellman, Elizabeth V. *Inessential Woman: Problems of Exclusion in Feminist Thought.* Boston: Beacon Press, 1988.

Tamez, Elsa. *Bible of the Oppressed.* Trans. Matthew J. O'Connell. Maryknoll, N.Y.: Orbis Books, 1982.

Weems, Renita J. *Just a Sister Away: A Womanist Vision of Women's Relationships in the Bible.* San Diego: LuraMedia, 1988.

World Council of Churches, Sub-unit on Women and Society. *By Our Lives...* *Stories of Women — Today and in the Bible*. Geneva: WCC Publications, 1985.

Chapter 2: PAINTING

Bennett, Anne McGrew. *From Women-Pain to Women-Vision: Writings in Feminist Theology*. Ed. Mary E. Hunt. Minneapolis: Fortress Press, 1989.

Borrowdale, Anne. *Distorted Images: Misunderstandings between Men and Women*. Louisville, Ky.: Westminster/John Knox Press, 1991.

Cooey, Paula M., Sharon A. Farmer, and Mary Ellen Ross, eds. *Embodied Love: Sensuality and Relationship as Feminist Values*. San Francisco: Harper & Row, 1987.

Duck, Ruth C. *Gender and the Name of God: The Trinitarian Baptismal Formula*. New York: Pilgrim Press, 1991.

Jantzen, Grace. *God's World, God's Body*. Philadelphia: Westminster Press, 1984.

Pauli Haddon, Genia. *Body Metaphors: Releasing the God-Feminine in Us All*. New York: Crossroad, 1988.

Saussy, Carroll. *God Images and Self Esteem: Empowering Women in a Patriarchal Society*. Louisville, Ky.: Westminster/John Knox Press, 1991.

Chapter 3: COOKING

Allison, Caroline. *"It's Like Holding the Key to Your Own Jail": Women in Namibia*. Geneva: WCC Publications, 1986.

Cannon, Katie G. *Black Womanist Ethics*. Atlanta: Scholars Press, 1988.

Pope-Levison, Priscilla, and John R. Levison. *Jesus in Global Contexts*. Louisville, Ky.: Westminster/John Knox Press, 1992.

Chapter 4: QUILTING

Davies, Susan E., and Eleanor H. Haney, eds. *Redefining Sexual Ethics: A Sourcebook of Essays, Stories, and Poems*. Cleveland: Pilgrim Press, 1991.

Farley, Wendy. *Tragic Vision and Divine Compassion: A Contemporary Theodicy*. Louisville, Ky.: Westminster/John Knox Press, 1990.

Halkes, Catharina J. M. *New Creation: Christian Feminism and the Renewal of the Earth*. Louisville, Ky.: Westminster/John Knox Press, 1991.

Primavesi, Anne. *From Apocalypse to Genesis: Ecology, Feminism, and Christianity*. Minneapolis: Fortress Press, 1991.

Chapter 5: WEAVING

Brown, Joanne Carlson, and Carole R. Bohn, eds. *Christianity, Patriarchy, and Abuse: A Feminist Critique*. New York: Pilgrim Press, 1989.

Plaskow, Judith, and Carol P. Christ, eds. *Weaving the Visions: New Patterns in Feminist Spirituality*. San Francisco: Harper & Row, 1989.

Stortz, Martha Ellen. *PastorPower*. Nashville: Abingdon Press, 1993.

Chapter 6: WELFARE

Abramovitz, Mimi. *Regulating the Lives of Women: Social Welfare Policy from Colonial Times to the Present.* Boston: South End Press, 1989.

Amott, Teresa, and Julie Matthaei. *Race, Gender and Work: A Multicultural Economic History of Women in the United States.* Boston: South End Press, 1991.

Couture, Pamela D. *Blessed Are the Poor? Women's Poverty, Family Policy, and Practical Theology.* Nashville: Abingdon Press; Washington, D.C.: Churches' Center for Theology and Public Policy, 1991.

Smith, Jackie M., ed. *Women, Faith, and Economic Justice.* Philadelphia: Westminster Press, 1985.

Chapter 7: REPRODUCTIVE CHOICES

Francome, Colin. *Abortion Freedom: A Worldwide Movement.* Boston: Allen & Unwin, 1984.

Luker, Kristin. *Abortion and the Politics of Motherhood.* Berkeley: University of California Press, 1984.

Messer, Ellen, and Kathryn E. May. *Back Rooms: Voices from the Illegal Abortion Era.* New York: St. Martin's Press, 1988.

Tickle, Phyllis, ed. *Confessing Conscience: Churched Women on Abortion.* Nashville: Abingdon Press, 1990.

Chapter 8: ADDICTION

Glaz, Maxine, and Jeanne Stevenson Moessner, eds. *Women in Travail and Transition: A New Pastoral Care.* Minneapolis: Fortress Press, 1990.

Hall, Nancy Lee. *A True Story of a Drunken Woman.* Boston: South End Press, 1990.

Kalant, Oriana Josseau. *Alcohol and Drug Problems in Women.* New York: Plenum Press, 1980.

Lebacqz, Karen. *Justice in an Unjust World: Foundations for a Christian Approach to Justice.* Minneapolis: Augsburg Publishing House, 1987.

Williams, Cecil, with Rebecca Laird. *No Hiding Place: Empowerment and Recovery for Our Troubled Communities.* San Francisco: HarperSanFrancisco, 1992.

Chapter 9: HANDICAPPING CONDITIONS

Browne, Susan, Debra Connors, and Nanci Stern, eds. *With the Power of Each Breath: A Disabled Women's Anthology.* Pittsburgh and San Francisco: Cleis Press, 1985.

Muller-Fahrenholz, Geiko, ed. *Partners in Life: The Handicapped and the Church.* Geneva: WCC Publications, 1979.

Presbyterian Church U.S.A. *That All May Enter: Responding to People with Disability Concerns.* Louisville, Ky.: Presbyterian Church U.S.A., 1989.

Chapter 10: CATASTROPHIC DISEASES

ACT UP/New York Women and AIDS Book Group. *Women, AIDS, and Activism.* Boston: South End Press, 1991.

Corea, Gena. *The Invisible Epidemic: The Story of Women and AIDS.* New York: HarperCollins, 1992.

Kübler-Ross, Elisabeth. *AIDS: The Ultimate Challenge.* New York: Macmillan Publishing Co., 1987.

O'Sullivan, Sue, and Kate Thomson, eds. *Positively Women: Living with AIDS.* London: Sheba Feminist Press, 1992.

Rudd, Andrea, and Darien Taylor, eds. *Positive Women: Voices of Women Living with AIDS.* Toronto: Second Story Press, 1992.

Sontag, Susan. *AIDS and Its Metaphors.* New York: Farrar, Straus & Giroux, 1989.